g lives

# Edexcel AS History [

## From Second Reich to Third Reich: Germany, 1918-45

Alan White

Series editors: Derrick Murphy and Angela Leonard

**STUDENT BOOK**

A PEARSON COMPANY

# Contents

# Introduction

Welcome to History at AS level. History is a fascinating subject, concerned with the world as it was and how it became the world we know now. By studying history, you will encounter new people, new places, new societies and cultures – even though they are all in the past. If you have an enquiring mind and an interest in the world around you then History is the subject for you.

## How to make the most of the course

- Practise your skills. History is not just about learning information or about telling the story of what happened in the past. You need to be able to understand and explain why things turned out the way they did and about how much they changed. The Skills Builder sections in this book will help you do this.

- Prepare for debate and discussion. Historians do not always agree about why events or developments in the past happened, or about their importance – so don't be afraid to debate with your teacher and other students. But remember that you must give evidence to support any point you make.

- Use the course book. This book has been designed to help you build up the skills, knowledge and understanding to help you do well in your exam – so use it. See the 'How this book will help you' section overleaf for details.

- Read around the subject. The more you learn about a period of history, the more interesting it becomes. Further reading on your chosen topics will broaden your understanding of the period, give you better insights into causation and change, and make the course much more rewarding.

## What you will learn

Unit 1 focuses on historical themes in breadth. This means that you need to be able to understand and explain why things changed over a fairly long period. In topic F7 you will learn about the troubled and violent history of Germany between the defeat of the Kaiser's Second Reich in 1918 and the destruction of Hitler's Third Reich in 1945. You will examine the circumstances in which the Second Reich was overthrown and replaced by a democratic republic in 1918–1919. You will study the democratic republic's struggle for survival in the 1920s in the face of attacks from anti-democratic forces in German society. You will learn about the growth of the Nazi Party and explore the reasons why it came to power. You will study the ways in which after 1933 the Nazis tried, with mixed success, to remodel German society and the German economy. You will also find out about the Nazi persecution of minorities. Finally, you will study the impact of war on Germany after 1939 and learn about the extent to which Hitler brought ruin on his people.

## How you will be assessed

For Unit 1 you will take a written exam. You will write two essays: one on each topic you have studied (i.e. one on Germany 1918–1945 and one on your other chosen topic). For each topic you will have a choice of two questions. You will have 1 hour and 20 minutes in total, or 40 minutes for each essay.

## How this book will help you

- Clearly written text gives you the historical information you need for this topic in the right amount of depth.

- 'Take note' boxes indicate when you should make notes of your own. These notes will help you with the activities and can also form the basis of your revision, so it's worth keeping up to date with these as you go along.

- Activities help you understand the content and build up your historical skills.

- Skills Builder sections help you develop the essential skills you need to do well in your exam.

- Examzone tells you what you need to know to prepare for the exam, including:
  - what to expect on the day
  - how to revise
  - what the assessment objectives mean and how you can meet them
  - what the different levels mean and how you can gain a high mark
  - example essays with examiner commentaries to help you understand what the examiners are looking for and how to use your information.

Pre-war Imperial Germany

# Chapter 1 Imperial Germany and its discontents

## Key questions

- How was Imperial Germany governed?
- How were the German economy and German society changing before 1914?
- In what ways, and how deeply, was pre-war German society divided?

'This war represents the German revolution.' This observation was made in the House of Commons in 1871 by the British Conservative politician Benjamin Disraeli. He was referring to Prussia's victory in its war against France and to the foundation of the German Empire which followed it. As Disraeli recognised, Germany was emerging as one of the world's most powerful states. The key to its growing strength was its economy. In the 50 years before the outbreak of war in 1914, Germany established itself as one of the world's industrial giants. Its achievements were, however, bought at a price. Pre-1914 Germany was not a country at ease with itself. The political and economic transformation which it underwent gave rise to internal divisions and tensions of a very serious kind. The most important divide within German society had to do with social class, but there were other sources of discord too, notably religion. These divisions shaped the course of German history, not only in the decades which preceded the First World War but in the years which followed it as well.

## The German Empire

### The political system

The German Empire, formed in 1871, was a union of 25 states of varying sizes: four kingdoms (Prussia, Bavaria, Saxony and Württemberg), six grand duchies, five duchies, seven principalities, and three free cities (Hamburg, Bremen and Lübeck). The Empire was not, however, an association into which all these states had entered on equal terms. Prussia, by far the largest and most powerful of the German states, pressurised the others into joining a Prussian-led empire. The process by which the German Empire was created is usually referred to as the unification of Germany, but **Prussification** might be a more accurate description.

Prussia dominated Imperial Germany at every turn. It accounted for two-thirds of the population of the German Empire. The Kings of Prussia, members of the Hohenzollern dynasty, became German **Kaisers**. Berlin, Prussia's capital city, became the capital of Germany. The Junkers, the Prussian landed aristocracy, were the most powerful social group in Imperial Germany. Prussia's supremacy unsurprisingly gave rise to resentment in other parts of Germany. In the lesser states there were those who dreamt of separating themselves from Prussia and regaining their pre-1871 independence.

### Glossary

**Prussification**

A term sometimes used by historians to refer to the dominant role of Prussia in the unification of Germany.

*Kaiser*

The German word for 'Emperor'. It comes from 'Caesar', a term used by the early Roman Emperors to describe themselves.

## Biography

### Wilhelm II
### (1859–1941)

Wilhelm II made it clear as soon as he became Kaiser that he was going to be a more hands-on monarch than his predecessors. He was in fact ill-suited to the business of government: he was unstable and erratic.

Wilhelm II in 1905

In some ways Imperial Germany looked like a democracy. All men over the age of 25 had the right to vote; there was a secret ballot; and new laws had to be approved by the Reichstag, the elected legislative body (see also Chapter 2, page 10). The Reichstag also had the power to accept or reject the budget. The Reichstag, however, had limited power over the government: the Kaiser had the power to appoint and dismiss government ministers without any reference to the Reichstag. In addition, the Kaiser had sole control over Germany's relations with other countries, undisputed command over Germany's armed forces and the power to dissolve the Reichstag whenever he chose. The Kaiser's powers, said one opposition politician, meant that the Reichstag was a mere 'sham parliament'. **Wilhelm II**, Kaiser between 1888 and 1918, certainly thought of himself as being in sole charge. 'There is only one master in Germany and that am I', he declared in the early 1890s. He added: 'Whoever opposes me I shall crush to pieces.'

### Economic growth

In the years 1871–1914 the German economy was the fastest-growing in Europe. During this period Germany's industrial production grew at twice the rate of France's and three times the rate of Britain's. By 1914 German industrial production had overtaken that of Britain.

Imperial Germany's economy was advanced and sophisticated as well as fast-growing. Its strengths lay in up-to-date industries, such as chemicals and electrical engineering. In these areas German companies became world-famous. One advantage they had was close links with Germany's renowned scientists. In the early part of the 20th century Germany was the scientific capital of the world. Its scientists left those of all other countries trailing in their wake when it came to winning Nobel Prizes. A good example of the way in which German industry benefited from German science is the Haber process, the basis of the modern fertiliser industry and one of the most important of all 20th century scientific discoveries. Professor Fritz Haber, who discovered the process in 1908, sold production rights to the BASF chemical company, which proceeded to make a fortune from them.

|  | 1871 | 1914 |
|---|---|---|
| Germany's population | 41 million | 66 million |
| Percentage of population living in towns of more than 100,000 people | 5% | 22% |
| Coal production (tons) | 47 million | 192 million |
| Steel production (tons) | 1.5 million | 18.6 million |
| Total length of railway track in Germany (in kilometres) | 24,000 | 55,000 |

Economic growth and social change in Germany, 1871–1914

## Imperial German society

### Working-class Germany

One of the most important consequences of Germany's rapid industrialisation was the growth of the working class. Living conditions for workers in Imperial Germany were grim. Wages were low, factory discipline was harsh and housing was notoriously bad. In Berlin, for example, workers were squeezed by the thousand into cramped and rat-infested 'rental barracks'. In these circumstances it is not surprising that the working classes turned to **socialism**. The Socialist Workers Party of Germany was formed in 1875, changing its name to the Social Democratic Party (SPD) in 1890. By 1914 it had developed into the biggest and best organised socialist party in Europe, with more seats in the Reichstag than any other party.

Imperial Germany's ruling class – the Junkers, the officer corps of the German army, the higher civil service, the industrial tycoons, and the leaders of the Protestant Church – feared and hated the SPD. In large part this was because the SPD's hostility to **capitalism** and its belief in equality represented a threat to their own wealth and status. These conservative elites, as they are sometimes called, lived in fear of a revolution. But there was another reason why they despised the SPD: because of its commitment to co-operation with foreign socialist parties they believed it to be unpatriotic. 'To me every Social Democrat is an enemy of the realm and of the Fatherland', declared Wilhelm II in 1889.

SPD supporters remained loyal to their party despite the hostility of the ruling elites. Their loyalty had much to do with the fact that the SPD offered its members a lot more than political representation. There existed under the SPD umbrella trade unions, newspapers, cultural organisations and sports clubs. The SPD was a way of life, not just a political party.

### Protestants and Catholics

Prussia was an overwhelmingly Protestant state. However, a number of the lesser states which joined the German Empire in 1871 were mainly Catholic, Bavaria being the biggest of them. The Rhineland and Silesia – two of Germany's most important industrial areas – were also largely Catholic. The Prussian ruling class viewed Catholics with suspicion because it was thought that in some circumstances they might prioritise their obedience to the Pope over their loyalty to Germany. These suspicions gave rise in the 1870s to the so-called *Kulturkampf* ('cultural struggle'), a series of measures designed to undermine the political influence of the Catholic Church in Germany. In self-defence, Germany's Catholics formed their own political party, the *Zentrum* or Centre Party. The Centre Party united Catholics of all social classes, from landowners to peasants and labourers.

The *Kulturkampf* was abandoned in the late 1870s, but Catholics in Germany remained to some degree second-class citizens. The numbers of Catholic students at Germany's universities were disproportionately low. Very few of Imperial Germany's top civil servants were Catholics.

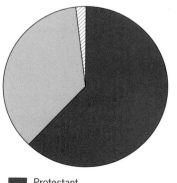

- Protestant
- Catholics
- Other

Protestants and Catholics in Germany, 1871

There were virtually no Catholics in the highest ranks of business or finance. Before 1914, Germany's Catholics were not enthusiastic supporters of the political system under which they lived.

**Taking it further**

If you want to find out more about Imperial Germany, a good starting-point is the online resource *German History in Documents and Images* (GHDI), an initiative of the German Historical Institute, Washington DC. In the document collection on *Wilhelmine Germany 1890–1918*, edited by Eric D. Weitz, find the Kaiser's 1891 speech to army recruits and the 1907 army report on domestic unrest: these will help you to understand what a tense and divided society Germany was in 1914.

## Conclusion: how was society divided in pre-war Germany?

German society before 1914 was divided into four main sub-cultures or 'camps'.

- At the top of the social pyramid was the conservative camp. The conservative camp was the ruling class of Imperial Germany.

- Arch-enemy of the conservative camp was the working-class camp, which had at its heart the SPD.

- Then there was the Catholic camp, alienated from Imperial Germany but also divided from the working-class camp by, among other things, socialism's association with atheism.

- Lastly, there was the middle-class camp, which was not as well-defined as the others because the German middle class was so diverse. The middle-class camp included intellectuals, members of professions such as law and medicine, businessmen and self-employed small tradesmen. Although there were critics of Imperial Germany to be found within this camp, most middle-class Germans accepted the Kaiser's rule despite their limited political role and influence.

## Activity: Imperial Germany and its critics

- The historian A.J.P. Taylor called Imperial Germany 'a dictatorship' but the historian James Retallack describes it as 'a semi-parliamentary monarchy'. Construct a two-column table, listing reasons which can be given in support of Taylor's view in one column and reasons which can be given in support of Retallack's in the other. In light of your table, which of these two views do you think is the more accurate?

- You are a British newspaper reporter in Germany in early 1914. You have to write a short article for your newspaper about the strengths, weaknesses and prospects of the Kaiser's regime. Remember to give your article a headline, and to write separate paragraphs on strengths, weaknesses and prospects.

- Produce an SPD poster for the Reichstag elections of 1912, which focuses either on what was wrong with the Kaiser's regime or on the ways in which the SPD wanted to change Germany.

# Chapter 2 **The German Revolution, 1918–1919**

## Key questions

- How and why did Imperial Germany collapse?
- How, after the Kaiser's abdication, did socialists disagree about Germany's political future in late 1918?
- Why did the use of the Free Corps in 1919 cause so much controversy?
- What were the weaknesses of the Weimar constitution?

When war broke out in 1914, the German people were told by their rulers that victory was certain. Four years later it appeared that the promised triumph was at hand. In March 1918 Russia's new Bolshevik government was forced to make peace with Germany. No longer fighting a war on two fronts, Germany reinforced its armies in France and launched the 'Ludendorff Offensive'. The anticipated breakthrough, however, did not materialise. American troops were arriving in France in large numbers. Not long after its tantalising glimpse of victory, Germany faced certain defeat. The credibility of Imperial Germany's ruling class was shattered: political change was inevitable. What followed was the German Revolution of 1918–1919. This was a complex affair which is best understood as a drama in three acts.

First, Germany's army commanders made an unsuccessful bid to impose a new political system on the country from above.

Second, moderate socialists took control of Germany's main cities and proclaimed the existence of a democratic republic.

Third, revolutionary socialists hostile to the idea of a democratic republic tried, but failed, to seize power through an armed uprising.

Out of this dramatic sequence of events emerged the Weimar Republic.

## Timeline

| | |
|---|---|
| **1 Oct 1918** | The 'revolution from above' |
| **4–8 Nov 1918** | Socialist-run **soviets** take control of Germany's major cities |
| **9 Nov 1918** | Abdication of the Kaiser; resignation of Prince Max; socialist government in power |
| **11 Nov 1918** | Fighting on the Western Front ended by the armistice |
| **6–11 Jan 1919** | 'Spartacus week' in Berlin: Communist revolt suppressed by Free Corps |
| **19 Jan 1919** | National Assembly elections |
| **May 1919** | Bavarian Soviet Republic overthrown |

## Glossary

**Soviet**

In the 1905 Russian revolution, factory workers spontaneously elected representatives to serve on city-wide strike committees. These committees became known as Councils of Workers' Representatives, or 'soviets' (councils) for short. It later became common to use the word to describe any locally-elected committee of workers' representatives.

**Take note**

As you work through the first part of this chapter, make notes to answer the following questions about political developments in Germany 1918-1919.
1 What were the main stages in the Kaiser's loss of political power in late 1918?
2 What were the main stages in the growth of the political influence of the moderate Social Democrats in late 1918?
3 Why was there so much political unrest in Germany in late 1918 and early 1919?

## The 'revolution from above', 1 October 1918

In September 1918 Germany's leading generals, **Ludendorff** and **Hindenburg**, told a stunned Kaiser Wilhelm II that the war was lost. Simultaneously, they urged him to appoint a new government made up of representatives of the biggest parties in the **Reichstag**. Reluctantly, the Kaiser agreed. At a stroke, Germany became a parliamentary democracy. The Kaiser would no longer have the power to appoint and dismiss ministers: governments would instead be answerable to the Reichstag. The Kaiser was to be nothing more than a ceremonial head of state.

The new Chancellor was Prince Max of Baden, widely respected as head of the German Red Cross but a political lightweight. The most important figures in the new government were the Social Democrat Philip Scheidemann and the Centre Party's Matthias Erzberger.

This 'revolution from above', as it became known, was on the face of things an astonishing development. Its architects, Ludendorff and Hindenburg, were no friends of democracy. The establishment of a parliamentary government and the appointment of socialist ministers ran contrary to everything they believed in. What prompted their action was the hope that a democratic Germany would get better peace terms from the victorious Allies than an **autocratic** one. They may also have hoped to divert attention away from their own responsibility for Germany's defeat by off-loading the blame onto Prince Max's government. Prince Max's ministers knew they might be held responsible for things that were not their fault but took office because they thought it their patriotic duty to do so.

**Take note**

As you read through this chapter, make notes about the roles played in the German revolution of 1918–1919 by Hindenburg, Liebknecht, Ebert and Noske. What sort of people in Germany in 1918–1919 would have been most critical of each of these individuals? What sort of criticisms would they have made of them? You might like to record your ideas in a table:

| Name | Role played | Critics and opponents | Criticisms |
|---|---|---|---|
| Hindenburg | | | |

## The popular revolution, November 1918

The 'revolution from above' was quickly overtaken by events. When Prince Max's government tried to open ceasefire talks with the Americans, it was told that Wilhelm II would have to step down before serious negotiations could begin. Inside Germany, demands for the Kaiser's abdication from his war-weary subjects grew ever louder.

Against this feverish background, Admiral Scheer, chief of the German naval staff, abruptly ordered the High Seas fleet to mount a last-ditch attack on the British. Apparently he saw such an attack as a matter of honour. Significantly, he saw no need to ask for clearance from Prince Max's government before issuing his order: he did not see himself as answerable to civilian politicians.

Scheer's recklessness triggered the next phase of the revolution. The sailors of the High Seas fleet had no enthusiasm for what they saw as a suicide mission and refused to obey orders. When the fleet returned to its base at Kiel on the Baltic Sea, the mutineers seized control of the port and set up an elected council of workers and soldiers – what in Russia was called a soviet – to run it.

In its prime, Imperial Germany would have responded swiftly and mercilessly to any whiff of mutiny within the armed forces. Brutal suppression would have been the order of the day. But no move to put down the Kiel mutiny was made. As a result, people across the country could see that Imperial Germany's ruling class had lost control and was no longer to be feared. Other German cities therefore followed where Kiel had led. Local councils, or soviets, dominated by socialists seized control of major cities like Hamburg, Cologne, Frankfurt, Munich and Berlin. By 9 November 1918 Germany, at the local level, was effectively being run by Social Democrats. At national government level there was confusion and uncertainty: the only thing that was clear was that large numbers of Germans did not want the Kaiser to remain even in a limited role as ceremonial head of state.

On 9 November 1918 Kaiser Wilhelm II bowed to the inevitable and abdicated. His departure opened the way for the armistice (ceasefire), which came into force two days later (11 November). Recognising that Germany's socialists were now in control, Prince Max also stood aside. A new six-man government made up exclusively of socialists then came into office. **Friedrich Ebert** was its most influential member. It was accepted on all sides that this could only be an interim government – after all, no one had elected it. Its task was to oversee the making of new, permanent arrangements for the government of Germany.

**Take note**

As you read through this section:
1. Produce a timeline of the key events in German politics between October 1918 and the National Assembly electons in January 1919.
2. Write a short paragraph explaining the part played in the German revolution of 1918-1919 by each of the following: the six-man interim government (known as the Council of People's Deputies) formed in November 1918; the December conference of delegates from the local soviets (which was known as the National Congress of Soviets); and the National Assembly elected in January 1919.

**Biography**

### Friedrich Ebert
### (1871–1925)

A former leatherworker who became a leading moderate Social Democrat, Ebert was in 1918–1919 the dominant figure within the six-man socialist government. He became President when Germany's new constitution came into effect. As President he was the target of endless upper-class sneers about his lowly social origins. Ebert was capable and well-intentioned but uncharismatic.

## Glossary

### Marxism

A variety of socialism associated with Karl Marx (1818–1880), which asserts that in industrial societies the working class, increasingly poverty-stricken and desperate, will inevitably rise up and overthrow the ruling class by revolutionary means.

### Communist

In his pamphlet the *Communist Manifesto* (1848), Karl Marx described his particular brand of revolutionary socialism as Communism. Political parties committed to Marxist ideas are therefore often referred to as 'Communist' parties.

### Bolsheviks

The revolutionary socialists who in October 1917 seized power in Russia.

## Socialist divisions

The SPD was the largest socialist party in the world in 1914 but it was also deeply divided. On paper the SPD was committed to **Marxism** and revolution but on the eve of war only a minority of its supporters were left-wing Marxists. The majority of Social Democrats were moderates – sometimes termed 'reformists' or 'revisionists' – who wanted to see socialist principles furthered by democratic methods.

The war added new divisions to those which already existed. Essentially, the moderate Social Democrats supported the war while left-wing socialists opposed it. In 1917 the anti-war minority broke away and formed a separate party, the Independent Socialists. However, this split did not prevent the Independents from agreeing to sit alongside moderate SPD leaders like Scheidemann and Friedrich Ebert in the six-man interim government which came into office in November 1918.

Loosely associated with the Independent Socialists in 1917–1918 was the Spartacus League, a group of hard-line Marxists. Named after the leader of a slave revolt in ancient Rome, the Spartacists were led by Karl Liebknecht, son of one of the founders of the SPD, and the brilliant Polish-born political theorist Rosa Luxemburg. At the beginning of 1919 the Spartacus League split away from the Independents and renamed itself the German **Communist** Party (KPD).

In the weeks after the Kaiser's downfall in November 1918 a frenzied debate took place among Germany's socialists on the question of the country's political future. There were two main options. The SPD moderates wanted the establishment of a democratic republic while the Spartacists envisaged the formation of a state controlled by the working class and its representatives – a state resembling Soviet Russia. The moderates pressed their case by proposing the election of a National Assembly, which would be given the task of drawing up a constitution for the new democratic Germany.

In December 1918 this proposal was debated at a major conference at which all of Germany's soviets were represented. Though known by a Russian name, Germany's soviets were nothing like their fiery **Bolshevik**-controlled counterparts in Petrograd and Moscow in 1917. Most of the soviets in Germany in 1918 were firmly under the control of SPD moderates. The outcome of the conference was therefore a foregone conclusion. It voted 344–98 in favour of the election of a National Assembly.

|  | Social democrats | Spartacus league (communists) |
|---|---|---|
| **Leaders** | Friedrich Ebert, Philip Scheidemann, Gustav Noske | Karl Liebknecht, Rosa Luxemburg |
| **Basic principles** | Democratic socialism | Revolutionary socialism |
| **Ideas about Germany's political future in 1918–1919** | Wanted a parliament elected by all of the German people to be the basis of the new political system. | Wanted a new political system based on local councils, or soviets, elected by the working class alone; middle and upper class Germans were to be given no say in how they were governed. |
| **Reason for disagreeing with the other's ideas** | Argued that imposing on Germany a political system based on councils elected by the workers alone was wrong because many Germans would be deprived of a say in how they were governed. | Argued that giving all Germans a vote in elections to parliament would hand control of Germany back to the middle and upper classes, who would then make sure Germany did not become a socialist country. |

Disagreements among Germany's socialists, 1918–1919

## The Spartacist challenge

The vote at the 1918 December conference of delegates from the local soviets left militant socialists in general, and Spartacists in particular, with a dilemma: they could either accept the conference's vote and allow a democratic Germany to be established without interruption, or they could seek to impose socialism on Germany by force.

The revolutionary option was obviously highly tempting, but in many ways the circumstances facing the Spartacists were unpromising.

- They had made no serious plans to seize power and were unprepared.
- Their leaders, Liebknecht and Luxemburg, were thinkers, not doers – theorists rather than decision makers.
- Numerically the Spartacists were weak.
- Powerful forces in Germany were working actively to undermine the appeal of revolutionary socialism. On 10 November 1918 the High Command of the German army agreed with the six-man socialist government to combat 'Bolshevism' in return for a government pledge to uphold discipline in the army. This agreement became known as the Ebert-Groener pact. A few days later, Germany's employers made significant concessions to the trade unions in the **Stinnes-Legien agreement**.

On the other hand, the Spartacists' position was by no means hopeless.

- They received backing from Lenin's Russia.
- They had the support of the radical trade union officials of Berlin's factories.
- There was widespread hunger and unrest in Germany linked to the continuing Allied naval blockade, which they could seek to exploit.
- Most important of all, the German army had disintegrated following the November armistice. This meant that the government could not rely on it to suppress a Spartacist revolt.

> **Take note**
>
> As you read through this section, make notes on why the Spartacist uprising failed.

> **The Stinnes-Legien agreement, 1918**
>
> Under this agreement, Germany's employers agreed to introduce an eight-hour working day, a long-standing trade union demand.
> Hugo Stinnes was an industrial tycoon and Carl Legien a prominent Social Democratic trade unionist.

### Biography

## Gustav Noske
### (1868–1946)

A one-time basket weaver who became an SPD member of the Reichstag in 1906. A practical man, he had little time for the intellectuals and theorists in his party. In early 1919 he famously described himself as 'the bloodhound' of the German revolution - meaning that he was ready to take on the task of tracking down and eliminating left-wing socialists who were a threat to democracy.

Gustav Noske in 1930

### Glossary

#### Mercenary

A soldier who fights in a war or other armed conflict in order to make money and is not motivated by any other consideration.

#### The Ruhr

The Ruhr area in the west of Germany was the country's most important industrial region. Its main industries were coal and steel. The area takes its name from one of the rivers, a tributary of the Rhine, which runs through it.

## The Free Corps and 'Spartacus week'

Recognising the army's unreliability, the government made contingency plans. **Gustav Noske**, the burly and forceful Defence Minister, authorised the formation of privately-organised military-style units to help maintain order. These were the so-called Free Corps (*Freikorps*). In all, over 150 separate Free Corps were formed involving around 400,000 men in total. Most originated from regular army units which had remained loyal to their officers, but there were civilian volunteers as well, many of them university students. Free Corps were often named after their commanders: examples include the 11,000-strong Hulsen Free Corps and the 5,000-man Ehrhardt Brigade. Men joined Free Corps for a variety of reasons. Some were straightforward **mercenaries**, but fear and hatred of revolutionary Marxism was a more common motivation. Free Corps volunteers certainly gained a reputation for brutality and right-wing extremism. Unsurprisingly, many of them later became members of the Nazi Party.

In early January 1919 the Spartacists organised anti-government demonstrations in Berlin. Encouraged by the size of the crowds that came out onto the streets, they raised the stakes, seizing control of government buildings and declaring that the government had been overthrown. The government's reply was to send Free Corps units into the capital. Better disciplined and more heavily armed than their opponents, the Free Corps crushed the Spartacists within a week. Liebknecht and Luxemburg, beaten to death by a Free Corps unit, were among the victims.

## The Free Corps unleashed

Following their success in Berlin, the Free Corps were let loose on other strongholds of revolutionary socialism in Germany. In the spring of 1919 they subdued the ports of Bremen and Hamburg and put down a general strike in **the Ruhr**. They then suppressed a further outbreak of Communist-led disturbances in Berlin. Their most violent campaign, however, took place in Bavaria. In late 1918 an independent socialist republic had been proclaimed in Bavaria. Its leader was Kurt Eisner, a radical socialist but not a Communist. In early 1919 Eisner was assassinated by a right-wing extremist. After his death, Bavaria shifted further leftwards: Communists took control and renamed Eisner's Bavarian Socialist Republic the Bavarian Soviet Republic. In May 1919 the Bavarian Soviet Republic was savagely overthrown by a 35,000-strong Free Corps army. At least 600 people were killed and many more were seriously wounded.

Upper-class Germans hailed the Free Corps as saviours, but revolutionary socialists hated them. Their hatred arose out of the brutality of the Free Corps. Revolutionary socialists also despised those who had unleashed the Free Corps on Germany. In their view, the moderate Social Democrats had sided with the worst elements of the ruling class of Imperial Germany against their own former comrades. To revolutionary socialists this alliance with enemies of the working class was a crime which could be neither forgiven nor forgotten.

The split which opened up in the German working-class movement was never to be closed.

## The Weimar constitution, 1919

The National Assembly elections for which the moderate Social Democrats fought so hard were held in late January 1919. Those political parties that, broadly speaking, favoured a democratic republic on principle won nearly 80 percent of all votes cast. These were the moderate Social Democrats; the Catholic Centre Party (*Zentrum*); and the newly-formed Democratic Party, whose support lay chiefly among the professional and educated middle classes. The Nationalist Party, representing big business and the Junkers, won only 10 percent of the vote. However, the 1919 election result was not such a sweeping endorsement of democracy as it might appear. Many middle-class Germans voted for the Democratic Party not out of democratic convictions but because they hoped that a Germany governed by moderates would be leniently treated by the Allies at the forthcoming Paris Peace Conference. In no subsequent Weimar election did the Democrats get anywhere near the 19 percent share of the vote that they won in 1919.

The task of the National Assembly was to draw up a new constitution for Germany. It started work in February 1919, not in bullet-riddled Berlin but in Weimar, a small central German city which had once been the home of Goethe, one of Germany's greatest writers. Here, protected by the Free Corps, the Assembly was able to deliberate in safety.

The constitution which emerged from the National Assembly's deliberations had three key features.

- It was an ultra-democratic constitution. The National Assembly went to great lengths to ensure that as much power as possible remained in the hands of the people. When the constitution came into force, Eduard David, a leading Social Democrat, declared Germany to be 'the most democratic democracy in the world'. (H.A. Winkler, 2006)

- It was a federal constitution. In federations, political authority is split between a national government and a number of state or provincial governments. The intention is to avoid an undue concentration of power in any one place and to give localities some control over their own affairs.

- At a national government level, the constitution was a mixture of a British-style parliamentary system and an American-style presidential system. In normal circumstances Germany was to be governed by ministers responsible to the Reichstag, but the President was given powers of his own, including the power to rule by decree in emergencies.

**Taking it further**

For those wishing to take the study of the Free Corps further, Chapter 1 of Richard J. Evans *The Coming of the Third Reich* (2003) is useful. There are also two informative short histories: Nigel Jones, *The Birth of the Nazis: How the Freikorps blazed a trail for Hitler* (2004) and Carlos Caballero Jurado, *The German Freikorps 1918–23* (2001).

| REFERENDUMS | NATIONAL GOVERNMENT | | | STATE GOVERNMENT |
|---|---|---|---|---|
| A referendum on a proposed law could be triggered by a petition signed by 10% of the electorate. | **REICH CHANCELLOR & REICH MINISTERS** The Chancellor was the head of the government. The Chancellor and government ministers were accountable to the Reichstag – meaning that governments could be removed from office by a hostile vote in the Reichstag. | **REICHSRAT** Represented the interests of the 17 states in the law-making process. Could veto (block) laws proposed by the Reichstag, but the Reichstag could override its veto. **REICHSTAG** The main law-making body. Its role was similar to that of the House of Commons in the British system of government. The Reichstag was elected every four years by proportional representation. | **PRESIDENT** Elected for 7 years. Head of state; commander-in-chief of armed forces; under Article 48 could in emergencies rule by decree. The President could be deposed by a referendum. | 17 states (or *länder*), each with its own government and elected parliament or *landtag*. Prussia was the biggest state by far. The powers of the states were limited and were largely confined to education, policing and religious affairs. |
| **CITIZENS' RIGHTS** Basic rights such as freedom of speech were guaranteed by the constitution. | | | | |

**ELECTORATE:** All Germans, men and women, over the age of 20. Women had not had the right to vote in Imperial Germany.

The Weimar constitution, 1919

**Proportional representation**

An electoral system which awards seats in parliament to political parties on the basis of the percentage share of the vote they win in elections.

**Article 48**

'If public security and order are seriously disturbed or endangered within the Reich, the President may take measures necessary for their restoration, intervening if need be with the assistance of the armed forces. For this purpose he may suspend, in whole or in part, fundamental rights.'

## Weaknesses of the Weimar constitution

It is sometimes claimed that the main weakness of the Weimar constitution – and one of the main reasons for the failure of the Weimar Republic – was the system of **proportional representation** used in Reichstag elections. Two arguments are put forward in support of this view. One is that proportional representation encouraged multi-party politics and by doing so ensured that Weimar governments were weak and unstable coalitions made up of several different parties. The other is that proportional representation made it easy for extremist parties to win seats in the Reichstag and gave them a platform they would not otherwise have had from which to attack the Weimar Republic.

These are not persuasive arguments. Proportional representation may have contributed to Germany's political woes after 1919 but it was certainly not their main cause. In the Weimar era there were a number of warring parties and the five or six biggest of them were capable of winning ten percent or more of the vote in national elections. However, this state of affairs owed far more to deep-rooted divisions in German society than it did to proportional representation. Germany would have had a problem with weak and unstable coalitions after 1919 whatever voting system had been adopted. What was true of the causes of political instability was also true of political extremism. The success of extremist political parties like the Communists and the Nazis in Weimar Germany owed far more to economic crises than it did to proportional representation.

The Weimar constitution's mixed parliamentary-presidential arrangement was a bigger source of difficulty than proportional representation. This arrangement worked well enough in the 1920s, but its defects became apparent in the early 1930s. **Article 48** of the constitution enabled the President to sideline the Reichstag and govern the country in 1930–1933 in a way that the constitution makers of 1919 had never envisaged.

They thought that crises requiring the use of Article 48 would last for days, not months or years. The real problem in the early 1930s, though, was not so much Article 48 itself but the existence of powerful people willing to exploit it. The Weimar constitution had its defects but it was not unworkable.

## Conclusion: how far did the 1918–1919 revolution transform Germany?

Late 1918 and early 1919 was undoubtedly a period of dramatic political change in Germany. Imperial Germany came to an end; a democratic republic was proclaimed; women received the right to vote. It would, however, be a mistake to think that the revolution of 1918–1919 transformed Germany completely. Alongside the changes which took place there were elements of continuity. Senior civil servants, police chiefs and judges who held office in Imperial Germany were allowed to remain in their posts, with the result that many key positions in German public life in the 1920s were occupied by people who were enemies of democracy. This was to prove a source of difficulty for the Republic. Neither did the revolution of 1918–1919 lead to huge changes in the distribution of wealth in German society. German banks and industries remained under private ownership. The rich remained rich and the poor remained poor.

## Activity: The failure of the extreme left, 1918–1919

- Work in groups to prepare a speech of about 300 words which might have been made in late 1918 by either a moderate Social Democrat or a Spartacist. The speech should explain and justify the speaker's views on how Germany should be governed. Speeches should include criticism of opponents' proposals as well as arguments in favour of the speaker's own suggestions.

- Present speeches to each other as a class.

- Which do you think is the more important reason for the failure of the extreme left in 1918–1919: its own internal weaknesses, or the toughness and determination of the moderate Social Democrats? Write a paragraph justifying your opinion.

## Activity: How democratic was the Weimar constitution?

- List ways in which the Weimar constitution could be said to be: (i) more democratic, and (ii) less democratic than the political system of Britain now. To what extent does your list support the conclusion that Weimar Germany was a more democratic democracy than 21st century Britain?

# Chapter 3  Democracy in crisis, 1919–1923

## Key questions

- Why did right- and left-wing extremists hate the Weimar Republic so much?
- Why were the extreme right able to make a political comeback in the early 1920s?
- Why was 1923 a year of crisis in Germany?
- Why did democracy in Germany survive the threats it faced in the early 1920s?

Extremists of the left *and* right hated the **Weimar Republic**. Reconciling themselves to it was unthinkable. What they hoped to do was destroy it. In early 1919 their chances of success appeared to be remote: the extreme right had been discredited by Germany's defeat and the extreme left had been crushed by the Free Corps. But the extremists of the right soon recovered. The key to their political comeback was the Treaty of Versailles. Much harsher than expected, the Treaty provoked outrage within Germany – outrage which the extreme right was able to exploit for its own ends. The issue of **reparations,** which arose out of the Treaty, gave the extreme right further ammunition with which to attack the Weimar Republic. The early 1920s saw a series of crises which took Germany's fledgling democracy to the brink of disaster.

## Glossary

### Weimar Republic

The name used by historians to refer to the democratic system of government which operated in Germany between 1918 and 1933. The name derives from the city where in early 1919 the National Assembly met to draft a new German constitution. In a republic the head of state is a president rather than a monarch.

### Reparations

These were payments which Germany had to make to the countries which had won the First World War to compensate them for the losses and damage they had suffered.

## Timeline

| Jun 1919 | Germany signed the Treaty of Versailles |
|---|---|
| Mar 1920 | The Kapp Putsch |
| 1921–1922 | Murders of Erzberger and Rathenau by Organisation Consul |
| Jan 1923 | French troops occupied the Ruhr |
| Sept 1923 | Germany called off its policy of 'passive resistance' |
| Nov 1923 | Hitler's 'Beer Hall Putsch' took place in Munich |

## The extreme right

### Who were the extreme right?

The extreme right's core support in the early years of the Weimar Republic came from the displaced ruling class of Imperial Germany – that is, from the Junkers, army officers and industrial tycoons.

The most important extreme right-wing political party in the 1920s was the German Nationalist Party (DNVP). It was monarchist, anti-democratic and anti-socialist: essentially what it wanted was a return to Imperial Germany. In elections it did well in eastern Germany, where the rural poor loyally voted for their Junker masters, but elsewhere it was an elite party rather than a mass party. On average it won 10 percent of the vote in the elections of the 1920s.

The extreme right may have had only limited electoral support but in other respects it was an extremely potent force. Its adherents had money and the influence which went with it. A key figure here was **Alfred Hugenberg**, leader of the Nationalist Party in the late 1920s. Hugenberg was a media tycoon who owned newspapers and publishing companies as well as Germany's most important film studio. He used the resources at his disposal to undermine the Republic in whatever ways he could.

A further strength of the extreme right was its capacity to bring armed forces into play. The early years of the Republic saw the formation of a large number of rightist **paramilitary forces**. One of the most prominent of these was the half-million strong *Stahlhelm*, nominally an ex-servicemen's organisation but in practice closely associated with the Nationalist Party. Apart from the paramilitaries, there was always the possibility that the regular German army, with its anti-democratic officer corps, would throw its weight behind attempts to overthrow the Republic.

## Why did the extreme right hate the Weimar Republic so much?

Three things account for the extreme right's deep and enduring hatred of the Republic.

- Before 1918 the extreme right had been Germany's ruling class. Extreme right-wingers resented the loss of the power and status they had come to think of as theirs by right.

- Extreme right-wingers viewed the Weimar Republic as the creation of those they regarded as the worst elements in German society – namely socialists, Catholics and Jews. To the extreme right, Weimar was a *Sozi-Republik* (Social Democratic Republic) and a **Judenrepublik** (Jewish Republic).

- Extreme right-wingers blamed Weimar politicians for Germany's defeat in the war. They claimed that these politicians – the 'November Criminals' as they branded them – had agreed to an armistice in 1918 even though Germany had been capable of fighting on. This claim was totally unrealistic. The extreme right nevertheless maintained that Weimar politicians were guilty of the *Dolchstoss* – the 'stab in the back'.

### *Judenrepublik*

Extreme right-wing propagandists claimed that Jews dominated the political life of the Weimar Republic and manipulated it in their own interests. Without regard for the truth, these propagandists exploited for all it was worth anything that happened which appeared to support their claim. An example was the Barmat scandal of 1924–1925, in which Jewish businessmen were accused of winning government contracts by bribing senior members of the Social Democratic Party.

### Glossary

**Paramilitary forces**

These are armed, uniformed military-style formations which resemble regular armies but which are privately organised and have no official status.

## The Treaty of Versailles, 1919

In early 1919 the victorious Allies gathered in Paris to discuss the terms of a final peace treaty with Germany. Three months later, a German delegation was sent for to be told what had been decided. A brief flurry of diplomatic activity ensued, after which Germany was given an ultimatum: agree to the Treaty within a week or face invasion.

The Treaty of Versailles plunged the Weimar Republic into crisis. Newspapers, church leaders and politicians of all parties united to condemn it, but Germany was not in a position to do anything but submit. Following an anguished debate in the Reichstag, Germany signed the Treaty of Versailles in June 1919 (see table).

---

**Main territorial provisions on Germany's western border**
- Alsace-Lorraine was returned to France, to which it had belonged before 1871.
- The Rhineland remained part of Germany, but became a demilitarised zone. This meant that Germany could not build fortifications or station troops within it. The western part of the Rhineland was to be occupied by Allied military forces for 15 years.
- The output of the Saar coalfield was to go to France for 15 years. This was to compensate France for the temporary loss of production from its war-damaged northern coalfields.

**Main territorial losses on Germany's eastern border**
- A strip of territory which became known as the 'Polish Corridor' was transferred to the newly created state of Poland to ensure that it had access to the sea.
- Germany also lost Memel (which subsequently became part of Lithuania) and Upper Silesia (to Poland). Danzig became a free city under League of Nations control.

**War guilt and reparations**
- Germany had to accept full responsibility for starting the war in 1914.
- Under the reparations settlement, Germany had to compensate the Allies for losses they had suffered during the war. The total sum due was not decided in 1919 but was fixed at £6,600 million by the Reparations Commission, which reported in 1921.

**Disarmament**
- The German army was restricted to 100,000 men and was not permitted to have tanks or heavy artillery.
- Germany was not allowed to have an air force.
- The German navy was permitted a limited number of ships, including six small battleships, but was to have no submarines.

**Colonies**
- Germany was stripped of the whole of its (relatively small) overseas empire.

---

The Treaty of Versailles, 1919: terms

## German objections to the Treaty of Versailles

Germans regarded the Treaty of Versailles as an outrage for a variety of reasons, but three stand out.

### The 'Diktat'

Germans objected to the manner in which the Treaty was made. They expected the armistice to be followed by a conference at which peace terms would be discussed between themselves and the Allies.

'Day of Versailles. Day of the dishonour'

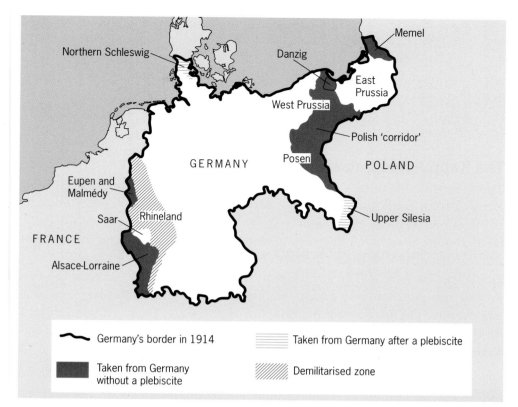

Germany's border in 1914

Taken from Germany without a plebiscite

Taken from Germany after a plebiscite

Demilitarised zone

Territorial changes in Europe under the Treaty of Versailles

They further believed that these discussions would be based on the Fourteen Points, a formula for a compromise peace which had been put forward by the American President, Woodrow Wilson, in January 1918. In the event, there were no discussions and little regard for the Fourteen Points. As a result, Germans believed they had been deceived. They branded the Treaty of Versailles a *Diktat* – a dictated peace.

## The war-guilt clause

Under Article 231 of the Treaty, the so-called 'war-guilt clause', Germany accepted sole responsibility for the outbreak of war in 1914 and for the suffering which followed. On the basis of the 'war-guilt clause' the Allies demanded reparations from Germany. In Germany, Article 231 was attacked as the 'war-guilt lie' and the reparations demands were seen as an Allied ploy to turn Germany into what one newspaper termed 'an economic corpse'.

## The 'Polish Corridor'

The establishment of the 'Polish Corridor' at Germany's expense aroused more bitterness than any of the other territorial losses. It placed more than a million Germans under Polish rule without their consent and it cut East Prussia off from the rest of Germany. These arrangements were seen in Germany as evidence of the Allies' hypocrisy: they said they believed in the right of **national self-determination** yet denied it to Germans in the 'Polish Corridor'. The strength of feeling in Germany about the 'Polish Corridor' can only be fully understood if it is borne in mind that many Germans viewed the Poles as a backward and primitive people. A phrase commonly used to describe Poles in 1920s Germany was *lausevolk* ('lice people').

### Glossary

**National self-determination**

The right of populations to decide for themselves the country to which they wish to belong rather than having a decision imposed upon them from outside.

The Treaty of Versailles was instrumental in reviving the fortunes of the extreme right. The extreme right's hard-line, aggressive nationalism went down well in a Germany which in mid-1919 was gripped by a mood of anger and dismay. The Treaty also helped the extreme right by discrediting democrats and Republicans: their belief that a democratic Germany would be more generously treated by the Allies than Imperial Germany was shown to be an illusion.

## The Kapp Putsch, 1920

The Treaty of Versailles – and in particular its limit on the size of the German army to 100,000 men – triggered the first right-wing attempt to overthrow the Republic by force. Immediately after the war, Germany's armed forces totalled more than half a million – 250,000 in the Free Corps and the rest in the regular army – so huge cuts were required in order to comply with the Versailles restrictions. The government therefore resolved to disband the Free Corps. But there was a complication: in 1919 Defence Minister Noske had promised to incorporate the Free Corps into the regular army in return for their efforts to defend the Republic. The government, however, pressed ahead with its plans.

In 1920 the Ehrhardt Brigade, the most notorious of the Free Corps, was ordered to disband. Its enraged commander, Hermann Ehrhardt, responded not only by refusing to obey the order but also by planning to topple the Republic which was responsible for it. He drew others into his plans, notably Walther von Lüttwitz, a senior general in the German army, and Wolfgang Kapp, an ultra-conservative politician. He then ordered his forces into Berlin and proclaimed the overthrow of the Republic. A shaken government left the capital and turned to the army for help. The army refused, its commander-in-chief, Hans von Seeckt, tersely informing the politicians that 'troops do not fire on troops'. The Kapp Putsch, though, petered out. Most on the extreme right saw it as a poorly organised affair and kept their distance from it. Berlin's civil servants refused to work for its leaders. In addition the Social Democrats organised a general strike in protest against it and brought Germany to a standstill. Ehrhardt, Lüttwitz and Kapp fled the country.

## Organisation Consul

A fanatic like Ehrhardt was never going to abandon the struggle against democracy easily. After the failure of the Kapp Putsch, he turned to political assassination as a means of destabilising the Republic. In 1921 he returned to Germany in secret and formed Organisation Consul, a right-wing death squad. Organisation Consul was responsible for the murder of Matthias Erzberger in 1921 and Walter Rathenau, Germany's Foreign Minister, in 1922. Erzberger was a marked man because he had negotiated the armistice in 1918: to the extreme right he was the leading 'November Criminal'. Rathenau was targeted in large part because he was Jewish. The murder of Rathenau led to a storm of protest in Germany and to a security crackdown which forced Organisation Consul to disband.

### Glossary

*Putsch*

A German word meaning an attempted seizure of power by force.

### Take note

As you work through this section, make notes which answer the following questions.
1. How serious a threat to the Weimar Republic were the extreme right and the extreme left?
2. Why did the extreme right and the extreme left fail to overthrow the Weimar Republic in the early 1920s?

## The threat from the extreme left in the early 1920s

The Communists' goal was a workers' state where power was concentrated in soviets (workers' councils), not the Reichstag. This was the fundamental reason for their opposition to Weimar democracy. But the events of 1918–1919 had given their hostility to the Republic an added edge. They believed that a socialist Germany had been within reach at the end of the war and were enraged by the way in which they had been thwarted. They were also embittered by the brutality with which Liebknecht, Luxemburg and others had been treated.

The Free Corps assault in 1919 left German Communism badly scarred but not fatally wounded. The German Communist Party (KPD) still had a sizeable following, especially among younger and less-skilled workers, and it inspired fanatical loyalty among its supporters. In 1920 it was boosted by the arrival of 400,000 new recruits who joined when the Independent Socialist party disintegrated. The German Communist Party's attempts to go on to the offensive, however, fared badly. In 1920 a Communist-led revolt in the Ruhr, Germany's most important industrial region, was crushed by the army. An attempt by the Communists to seize power in Saxony in 1921 ended in similar fashion. The extreme left was not as deadly an opponent of the Republic as the extreme right: it did not have the same ability to influence public opinion and it had fewer armed men to call upon. In addition, the extreme left was often treated more harshly by the authorities than the extreme right. This was due in large part to the fact that members of the pre-war elites – who feared revolutionary socialism above all – continued to hold key positions in government and the judicial system.

## The crisis of 1923

In the course of 1923, the Weimar Republic's fortunes went from bad to worse. In January France sent troops into the Ruhr; by the summer the country was in the grip of catastrophic **hyperinflation**; and in the autumn both the extreme left and the extreme right began to move in for the kill.

### What caused hyperinflation?

The crisis of 1923 had its origins in France's dissatisfaction with the Treaty of Versailles. The French believed that the Treaty had failed to provide them with long-term security against the threat of German aggression. As a result, they adopted a policy of ultra-strict enforcement of the terms of the Treaty. The aim was to keep Germany in a permanently weakened condition. When Germany in early 1923 failed to make a reparations payment on schedule, France responded by occupying the Ruhr.

Shorn of its military strength by the Treaty of Versailles, Germany was in no position to resist the French by force. It opted instead for a policy of passive resistance aimed at bringing the Ruhr to a standstill and preventing France pillaging its wealth. The Ruhr's industrial workers were instructed to go out on strike, with the German government promising to compensate them for their lost wages.

**Take note**

As you read through this section, make a bullet-point list of the causes of hyperinflation and a mind map of the effects of hyperinflation for the different sections of German society.

**Glossary**

### Inflation and hyperinflation

Inflation means rising prices or – to put the same thing in a different way – a fall in the purchasing power of money. Hyperinflation is inflation which is very high or out of control.

### ...ency speculators

...n Germany in 1923 these were typically businessmen and financiers who used borrowed money to buy foreign currencies like the dollar. The value of the dollar rose while that of the German mark fell.

## Biography

### Hugo Stinnes
(1870–1924)

The Ruhr industrialist Hugo Stinnes was the most successful currency speculator in Germany in 1923, using his profits to enlarge his already vast business empire. In Germany he became known as 'the Inflation King' and an American magazine called him 'the New Emperor of Germany' (see also the Stinnes-Legien agreement page 13, Chapter 2).

Germany's finances were in a mess even before the start of 'passive resistance'. It had paid for the 1914–1918 war largely by borrowing rather than by increasing taxes – the expectation being that lenders, most of them ordinary Germans, would be repaid out of reparations imposed on the defeated Allies. In 1918 Germany was left with an acute debt problem. It was a problem which became very much worse when the Allies demanded £6,600 million in reparations in 1921. Nor did Germany's woes end there: indebtedness had a toxic by-product in the shape of rampant inflation. The value of the German mark in relation to other currencies declined as the world's money markets lost faith in it. As a result, Germany had to pay more for its imports in the early 1920s, and this drove up the cost of living.

Passive resistance turned rampant inflation into hyperinflation. A huge gap opened up between rising government spending – the result of payments to the striking Ruhr workers – and its falling income from taxation. Tax receipts fell because of rising unemployment: with the Ruhr at a standstill, businesses in other parts of Germany which supplied it scaled down their operations. The government's answer to its budget deficit – the gap between income and spending – was to print paper money. This policy destroyed what was left of confidence in the German mark and led to its total collapse. By the autumn of 1923 loaves of bread, which had cost half a mark in 1918, were selling at more than a billion marks. The mark was losing value not weekly or daily but hourly. In the end, people gave up on paper money and resorted instead to barter – exchanging goods for goods. Signs could be seen offering cinema admission in return for two lumps of coal. 'The condition of Germany today beggars description', wrote a British newspaper correspondent in October 1923.

### Hyperinflation: winners and losers

Hyperinflation meant misery for most Germans. A minority, however, profited from it. The biggest losers from hyperinflation were to be found within the middle classes. These people believed they had been betrayed by the Weimar Republic.

| Winners | Permanent losers | Temporary losers |
|---|---|---|
| People who owed money and who paid off their debts in worthless currency.<br>• Examples included industrialists who had borrowed money to invest in their factories and landowners who had mortgaged their estates.<br>• **Currency speculators** like **Hugo Stinnes** also gained from hyperinflation.<br>• Most of these winners belonged to the wealthiest sections of German society. | People who had saved money and saw the value of their savings wiped out by hyperinflation. Those who lost out in this way were not compensated.<br>• Examples included: people with money in bank accounts; people who had invested in insurance policies and pension schemes; people who had lent the government money in the 1914–1918 war.<br>• Most people in this category were middle class. | People who neither owed money nor had much in the way of savings, but whose wages failed to keep pace with inflation as 1923 wore on.<br>• People in this category suffered badly in the short term in late 1923 because they found it increasingly difficult to obtain food, but recovered quickly once the currency was stabilised and did not suffer ill effects in the long term.<br>• Most people in this category were working class. |

The impact of hyperinflation

## Political unrest

In early 1923, thanks to the trade unions, wages mostly kept up with rising prices, shielding working-class Germans from the worst effects of inflation. In mid-1923, however, prices started to surge ahead of wages, making it difficult for poorer families to buy food. Barter was not really an option for these families: being poor, they had few goods to offer in exchange for food. By the autumn of 1923, hyperinflation had reduced the working class to a state of desperation. Serious unrest occurred in the poorer districts of Germany's cities in the form of strikes, hunger riots and looting. These were conditions tailor-made for the Communists of the KPD. With support from Soviet Russia, it made plans first to seize control of Saxony and then to use Saxony as a springboard from which to take over the rest of Germany.

The events of 1923 also played into the hands of the extreme right. The French occupation of the Ruhr gave rise to an intensely nationalistic mood in Germany which the extreme right was well placed to exploit. They also exploited middle- and upper-class fears of a Communist *putsch*. The abandonment of passive resistance in September 1923 strengthened the extreme right's position further by allowing it to claim that the Republic had capitulated to the French. Unsurprisingly, prominent right-wing extremists – Hugenberg, Stinnes, von Seeckt and Ludendorff among them – began at this point actively to consider a *putsch*. Their plans involved using Bavaria – where **Gustav von Kahr**, another rightist, headed the state government – as the launching-pad for a march on Berlin. In Munich, Bavaria's capital, von Kahr began to assemble paramilitary forces for the purpose.

In September 1923 a crisis government involving all of Germany's democratic parties came into office. At its head, as Chancellor, was Gustav Stresemann of the **German People's Party (DVP)**. In October 1923 Stresemann's government took decisive action against the Communists in Saxony, ordering the army in to take control. With the extreme right, Stresemann opted for a waiting game. The rightists dithered. In Munich, Hitler's **Nazis**, bit-part players in von Kahr's plans, tried to prod him into action by a show of force. This was the so-called 'Beer Hall Putsch'. It was brought to an end when police units loyal to von Kahr opened fire on Nazi marchers, killing 14 of them. Four policemen also died. Once again the extreme right had been undermined by internal divisions.

### The Nazi Party

The National Socialist German Workers' Party (NSDAP) – known as the Nazi Party – was founded under the leadership of Adolf Hitler in Munich in 1920. In the early 1920s it was one of a large number of extreme right-wing groups competing for support in Bavaria.

**Taking it further**

Any attempt to explain the survival of the Republic in 1919-1923 has to take into account the fact that there were Germans who wanted it to succeed and that at some points its supporters acted robustly in its defence. Read the account of these years in Ruth Henig, *The Weimar Republic* (London, 1998) or any other in-depth study of the Weimar Republic and make lists of (i) evidence which suggests there was popular support for the Republic and (ii) instances where supporters of the Republic acted robustly in its defence.

## Conclusion: how can the survival of the Republic in the early 1920s be explained?

The extreme left failed in 1919–1923 mainly because it lacked popular support. Only a minority of the German working class sided with it. The extreme right lacked widespread popular support too, but its failure perhaps owed more to its internal divisions. At no point in 1919–1923 did it attack the Republic in a concerted fashion, bringing all of the resources available to it into play. The Weimar Republic did not, however, survive these years of turmoil only because its enemies had weaknesses. There was in Germany a sizeable body of opinion, with the SPD and its followers at its core, which was firmly committed to the democratic experiment.

## Activity: Threats to the Republic, 1919–1923

- Rank the following five extreme right-wingers 1–5 in order of their importance as enemies of the Republic in 1919–1923, giving reasons for your ranking: Alfred Hugenberg; Hermann Ehrhardt; Hans von Seeckt; Gustav von Kahr; Adolf Hitler.

- Copy and complete the diagram below by adding boxes which give evidence in support of the three reasons given for the failure of the extreme right to overthrow the Republic.

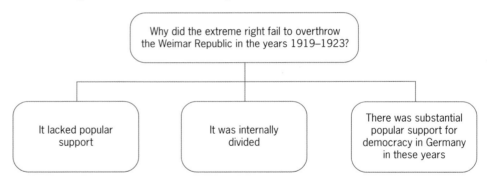

Why did the extreme right fail to overthrow the Weimar Republic in the years 1919–1923?

| It lacked popular support | It was internally divided | There was substantial popular support for democracy in Germany in these years |

- Under the heading 'The Treaty of Versailles as a cause of unrest in Germany 1919–1923', write two short paragraphs, one headed 'Direct effects' and the second headed 'Indirect effects'. Include in your first paragraph references to the impact of restrictions on the size of the army and of reparations, and in your second include references to the way in which the Treaty brought about a revival of the extreme right and damaged the reputation of the Republic.

# Chapter 4 Stresemann and stability, 1924–1929

## Key questions

- In what ways, and how significantly, did Stresemann, as Chancellor and Foreign Minister, contribute to Germany's recovery after 1923?
- Why did Stresemann polarise opinion in Germany?
- How stable was the Weimar Republic on the eve of the Great Depression?

The later 1920s were a period of relative calm in Germany. The economy picked up and the extremist threat appeared to recede. This upturn in Germany's fortunes owed much to the work of one man – **Gustav Stresemann**. Stresemann, who was Chancellor in 1923 and Foreign Minister between 1924 and 1929, was the one outstanding statesman of the Weimar era. Most of the Republic's political leaders were well-intentioned but uninspiring. Ebert is a case in point. Stresemann was different: he was shrewd, imaginative and courageous. As Chancellor, he led Germany out of the hyperinflation crisis. As Foreign Minister, his skilful diplomacy ended Germany's isolation within the international community and made Germany a magnet for foreign investment. It might be thought that his achievements would have won him universal acclaim within Germany. They did not. Stresemann was a highly controversial figure – admired by some, reviled by others.

## Timeline

| | |
|---|---|
| **1923** | End to passive resistance; introduction of the *Rentenmark* |
| **1924** | Dawes Plan |
| **1925** | Locarno Pact |
| **1926** | Germany admitted to the League of Nations; Gustav Stresemann awarded the Nobel Peace Prize |
| **1927** | Unemployment Insurance Act |
| **1928** | Reichstag elections: extreme right-wing parties lost ground |
| **1929** | Young Plan; Stresemann's death aged 51 |

## Biography

### Gustav Stresemann

(1878–1929)

Born into a lower-middle-class Berlin family, Stresemann entered the Reichstag in 1907, aged only 28, and went on to build a reputation as a moderate conservative. In 1914–1918 he moved to the right, aligning himself with supporters of an all-out war policy and demanding big territorial gains for Germany at the expense of France, Belgium and Russia as part of any peace settlement. Initially, Stresemann was an enemy of the Republic: he described himself as a monarchist and, along with his party, the German People's Party (DVP), voted against the constitution in the 1919 National Assembly. He also failed to come out against the Kapp Putsch in 1920. Subsequently Stresemann made his peace with the Republic, mostly because he reached the conclusion there was no workable alternative to it.

Stresemann in 1929

## What did Stresemann achieve as Chancellor?

Stresemann was Chancellor for a little over three months in late 1923. In this brief period, though, he did his country three enormous services.

- He called off passive resistance in the Ruhr. This decision was inevitable – the costs of passive resistance had become unbearable – but that did not make it any easier. Stresemann knew that when he called off passive resistance he would come under ferocious attack from the extreme right: he told his wife he would be committing political suicide. He nevertheless went ahead. The decision to abandon passive resistance was proof of Stresemann's political courage.

- He oversaw the introduction of a new currency to replace the worthless mark. The new currency – known first as the *Rentenmark* and then as the *Reichsmark* – was issued in strictly limited quantities so that it would retain its value. One trillion old marks were exchangeable for one *Rentenmark*. The establishment of a stable currency paved the way for the return of normal economic life: people no longer had to rely on barter.

- He fended off threats to the Republic's survival from the extreme left and the extreme right. He defeated the Communists by ordering the army into Saxony and overcame the extreme right by waiting until it self-destructed in Bavaria in the ill-fated Munich Beer Hall Putsch of November 1923 (see also page 39, Chapter 5).

The extent of Stresemann's achievement is not to be underestimated. In late 1923 the Republic's future hung in the balance. Many Germans believed that it would not survive. Some expected that its collapse would be followed by a left–right civil war. Under intense pressure, Stresemann steered Germany through the most difficult phase of the 1923 crisis in an astute and sure-footed way.

Stresemann received little gratitude for his efforts. His policies as Chancellor not only angered his enemies outside the government but also his partners within it. Upset by the contrast between the harsh treatment of the left in Saxony and the comparative restraint shown towards the extreme right in Bavaria, the Social Democrats left the government. Stresemann was forced to resign the Chancellorship.

## Stresemann's foreign policy: aims and methods

German foreign policy in the 1920s revolved around the Treaty of Versailles. Opinion in Germany on what to do about the hated *Diktat* differed. One approach, favoured by the extreme right, involved refusing to obey the Treaty and daring Germany's enemies to do their worst. Its critics saw this as an insane 'disaster policy'. The other main approach, pioneered by Rathenau, the Foreign Minister assassinated in 1922, and pursued by Stresemann, was more subtle. It involved trying to improve relations with the Allies in the belief that they could then be persuaded to make significant changes to the Treaty of Versailles. This approach was known as the policy of **fulfilment**.

### Glossary

**Fulfilment**

A term used to describe the foreign policy advocated by Rathenau and Stresemann which involved Germany meeting its obligations under the Treaty of Versailles, in particular by paying reparations. The assumption was that, if Germany showed willing, the Allies could in due course be persuaded to alter the terms of the Treaty in major ways.

This was because Germany, as part of its tactic of winning the confidence of France and Britain, fulfilled its obligations under the Treaty to pay reparations. Extreme right-wingers saw the 'fulfilment policy' as an outrage. They claimed that by paying reparations Germany was in effect accepting the 'war-guilt lie'. Stresemann was unmoved. His view was that Germany's military weakness meant that fulfilment was its only option. Without raw power to fall back on, he said, Germany had to rely on clever diplomacy to advance its interests.

Stresemann's attempts to improve relations between Germany and its enemies led some to see him as a soft-centred idealist who wanted reconciliation between states for its own sake. He was no such thing. He was a German nationalist and a hard-headed realist. Reconciliation was a means to an end. The ends Stresemann sought were the revision of the Treaty of Versailles in Germany's favour and the restoration of its great power status. In 1924 his immediate aims were to get the French out of the Ruhr and reparations scaled down. In the longer term he hoped to regain the Polish Corridor and maybe Germany's lost colonies.

> **Take note**
>
> As you read through this section, make bullet-point notes summarising (i) the arguments which Stresemann and the extreme right each put forward in support of their ideas on foreign policy, and (ii) the reasons why each criticised the other.

| Achievement | What was involved? | How did Germany benefit? |
|---|---|---|
| Dawes Plan, 1924 | The Dawes Plan was a stop-gap agreement about reparations between Germany and the Allies, named after a US banker who helped draft it. Germany agreed to resume reparations payments in return for a reduction in the amount payable each year. However, to ensure payments took place, the Allies insisted on arrangements which allowed them to supervise Germany's national bank. | • Part of the deal was that French forces would end their occupation of the Ruhr.<br>• Germany received a sizeable loan ($200 million) from the USA to help it restart reparations payments. |
| Locarno Pact, 1925 | France and Germany agreed not to change by force the border between the two countries laid down by the Treaty of Versailles. However, no agreements were made about Germany's eastern borders with Austria, Czechoslovakia and Poland. | • The pact involved France promising not to repeat the occupation of the Ruhr, with Germany in return giving up any claim to Alsace-Lorraine – a good deal for Germany because it had no real designs on the area anyway.<br>• Part of the deal was that Germany would be admitted to the League of Nations, bringing to an end its 'outsider' status within the international community. |
| Young Plan, 1929 | An agreement between Germany and the Allies about reparations, named after the American who chaired the negotiations leading to it, which replaced the 1924 Dawes Plan and was intended to be a final settlement of the reparations issue. | • Germany's total reparations liability was reduced from the £6,600 million demanded in 1921 to £1,850 million – a reduction of more than two-thirds.<br>• The Allies agreed to remove their forces from the western part of the Rhineland five years ahead of the schedule laid down by the 1919 Treaty of Versailles – enabling Stresemann to declare that Germany was now free of all foreign occupying forces. |

Stresemann's diplomacy, 1924–1929: principal achievements

**Take note**

As you read through this section, construct a two-column table listing (i) the strengths and (ii) the weaknesses of the German economy in the later 1920s.

## The later 1920s: a booming economy?

In the later 1920s the German economy returned to something approaching normality. Rid of hyperinflation and no longer isolated within the international community, Germany became highly attractive to foreign investors. Money flowed into the country, especially from the United States. This influx of capital enabled businesses to upgrade their plant and machinery and local councils to finance vast house-building schemes. The economy grew, with industrial output returning to pre-war levels in 1928. Wages went up too, with trade unions often bargaining successfully on behalf of their members. Another feature of the later 1920s was people's inclination to spend rather than save – something which helped to create the impression that there was plenty of money around. Like the United States, Germany had its 'roaring twenties'.

High levels of consumption did not, however, mean that Germany had been restored to full economic health. In some respects the German economy in the later 1920s was seriously unstable. It was also undermined by tensions and conflicts between different economic stakeholders.

- Germany's prosperity was heavily dependent on foreign investment, much of which took the form of loans and credits which could be withdrawn at short notice. In particular, the Dawes and Young Plans linked the German economy closely to that of the USA, which brought serious consequences for Germany after the Wall Street Crash of 1929 (see Chapter 6).

- The agricultural sector of the economy did not share in the general prosperity. World food prices were low in the later 1920s and farmers' incomes suffered as a result. Unable to make ends meet, farmers went heavily into debt and bitterly resented the failure of the Republic to do more to help them.

- In some of the country's biggest industries there was a lot of friction between employers and workers. Employers believed that the unions had too much power and that wages were too high as a result. Adopting a confrontational approach, they tried to reduce their workforces by introducing labour-saving machinery. The trade unions did not surrender without a fight. Strikes and lock-outs were frequent.

- Governments lived beyond their means. Public spending was higher than the government's income from taxation. The gap between the two – the budget deficit – was covered by borrowing. High levels of borrowing could not be sustained indefinitely.

|  | Dec 1924 | 1928 |
|---|---|---|
| Nationalists | 21% | 14% |
| SPD | 26% | 30% |
| Nazis | 3% | 2% |

SPD gains and extreme right-wing losses in the 1928 Reichstag elections

## The later 1920s: political stability?

A measure of calm returned to political as well as to economic life in the later 1920s. The extremists no longer had hunger and desperation off which to feed. Political moderates could reflect with satisfaction on the absence of *putsch* attempts in the later 1920s and on the heavy losses suffered by the parties of the extreme right in the Reichstag elections of 1928.

In some ways, though, the appearance of calm was misleading. The Republic remained an unstable political system with an uncertain future.

- One important reason for the Republic's continuing fragility was middle-class disillusionment with it. Still reeling from the impact of hyperinflation, middle-class Germans in the later 1920s frequently complained of being treated unfairly in comparison with the working classes. They saw working-class interests being furthered by local government house-building and the **Unemployment Insurance Act** of 1927 and felt that no comparable attempt was being made to look after them. The Republic, they claimed, had become a 'trade union state'. Evidence of middle-class disillusionment with the Republic in this period includes the election of Hindenburg, an avowed anti-democrat, as President in 1925 and the growth of middle-class protest parties, notably the Economy Party, which in the 1928 elections won nearly 5 percent of the vote.

- The extremist threat did not wither away. What happened instead was that the extremists, learning from their failures to seize power by force, varied their tactics. The Nazis and the Communists, the latter under the leadership of **Ernst Thälmann**, both started to contest Reichstag elections in earnest. Both tried as well to destabilise the Republic through street violence. By the late 1920s a week rarely went by in which there were no major clashes between the **SA**, the Nazi paramilitary organisation, and its Communist counterpart, the Red Front Fighters' League.

## Biography

### Ernst Thälmann
(1886–1944)

Unlike his predecessors, Liebknecht and Luxemburg (both middle-class intellectuals), the tough, leather-jacketed Thälmann had a working-class background: before 1914 he worked as a merchant seaman. As leader of German Communism in the 1920s, Thälmann saw himself more than anything else as a servant of the interests of Soviet Russia: he turned the KPD into a Stalinist party which obeyed whatever instructions it received from Moscow. In 1922 Thälmann survived an Organisation Consul assassination attempt; in 1933 he was imprisoned by the Nazis; in 1944, with the end of the war in sight, he was murdered by the Nazis in Buchenwald concentration camp.

## Why was Stresemann such a controversial figure?

Stresemann was a politician who polarised opinion. His greatest admirers were to be found among Germany's political moderates: his deadliest enemies were on the extreme right.

Political moderates in the Social Democratic, Centre and Democratic parties did not agree with all of Stresemann's views on domestic policy, but they respected his political courage.

### The Unemployment Insurance Act, 1927

The beginnings of a welfare state were established in Germany in the 1880s with the introduction of old age pensions and a health insurance scheme. The 1927 Act built on these foundations by introducing arrangements under which workers and employees contributed to a fund out of which benefits were paid to jobless workers. The 1927 Act was one of the most important laws passed by the Reichstag in the Weimar era.

### Glossary

### The SA

The Nazi SA (*Sturmabteilung*, or storm troop) was named after the elite units of the German army in the 1914-1918 war which led assaults on enemy trenches. Because of the uniform they wore, Nazi SA men were often referred to as 'Brownshirts'.

They applauded his foreign policy, recognising that it produced gains for Germany which a lesser diplomat could not have secured. A further reason for admiring Stresemann was the belief that he had moved leftwards in the course of his political career, abandoning the aggressive nationalism of his youth in favour of a more conciliatory and statesmanlike approach to international affairs.

Stresemann's career path was one of the reasons extreme right-wingers despised him: they saw him as a turncoat, someone who had deserted the nationalist cause and thrown his lot in with enemies of the fatherland. The extreme right also opposed Stresemann's 'fulfilment policy' on principle, claiming that it meant negotiating with Germany's enemies when they should have been defied. Extreme right-wing propaganda made much of the concessions Germany made in connection with the Dawes and Young Plans – notably the agreement under the Young Plan to make 58 annual reparation repayments, the last not being due until 1988. This, claimed the extreme right, meant that generations of Germans as yet unborn would be 'enslaved'. Just before Stresemann's premature death in 1929, the extreme right forced a referendum on a law which, if passed, would have seen him branded a national traitor. When the referendum took place, however, the extreme right was heavily defeated, with only 14 percent of voters supporting its proposal.

## Conclusion: how far was Stresemann responsible for the upturn of the later 1920s?

### The 'golden years'

One thing which was golden about the Weimar Republic was its cultural life. The dazzling array of talent at work in Germany in the 1920s included the writers Thomas Mann and Bertolt Brecht, the artists George Grosz and Käthe Kollwitz and the film-makers Fritz Lang and Joseph von Sternberg. Many of Weimar Germany's artists were on the left politically and were attacked by the extreme right as corrupt and unpatriotic.

The later 1920s are sometimes described as the 'golden years' of the Weimar Republic. In view of Germany's continuing economic and political difficulties this is too generous a verdict, but things were undoubtedly better than they had been in the years of turmoil up to 1923. Stresemann deserves a lot of the credit for the gains which were made, but it is wrong to think that he revived Germany's fortunes single-handedly. Others made significant contributions too.

- Rathenau, not Stresemann, originated the 'policy of fulfilment'.

- President Ebert made extensive use of his emergency powers in 1923 with the aim of keeping the Republic afloat.

- The introduction of the *Rentenmark*, an exercise of huge complexity, was not primarily the work of Stresemann, but of two financial experts: Hans Luther, the Finance Minister, and Hjalmar Schacht, banker and Reich Currency Commissioner. Schacht also played an important part in negotiating the Dawes and Young Plans.

- Stresemann operated throughout his ministerial career in coalition governments made up of three or four different parties. He depended on his coalition partners to give him room to manoeuvre.

Stresemann's diplomacy would have got nowhere without Britain and France being willing to accommodate him and the USA being prepared to involve itself in the talks which led to the Dawes and Young Plans.

It also needs to be borne in mind that Stresemann's diplomacy had its limitations. He made no progress towards regaining the Polish Corridor or Germany's lost colonies. Nor was the economic recovery his diplomacy helped to bring about built on solid foundations. Stresemann admitted as much himself. 'The German economy is doing well only on the surface', he said in a speech in 1929. 'Germany is in fact dancing on a volcano. If the short-term loans are called in by America, most of our economy will collapse.'

## Activity: Weimar's 'golden years'?

- As a class, divide into three groups. Each group is to produce a brief obituary of Stresemann for a different German newspaper: an extreme right-wing newspaper; a newspaper which supported Stresemann's own party, the People's Party; and a Social Democratic Party newspaper. An obituary is a short biography assessing the character and achievements of someone which appears after his or her death. Each group should present its obituary to the others and defend it against criticisms.

- Produce two slides for use in a PowerPoint presentation, one indicating what reasons there were in 1924–1929 for optimism about the Weimar Republic's survival prospects, the other showing what reasons there were for pessimism.

- 'The Weimar Republic was just as unstable in the later 1920s as it was in the early 1920s.' To what extent would you agree with this claim?

**Taking it further**

If you want to find out more about Gustav Stresemann, two accessible articles are Jonathan Wright, 'Gustav Stresemann, Weimar's Greatest Statesman', *History Today* (November 2002), and E.J. Feuchtwanger, 'Hitler, Stresemann and the Discontinuity of German Foreign Policy', *History Review* (December 1999). Consider in particular what these articles have to say about Stresemann's aims and about the reasons why he was a controversial figure.

# Skills Builder 1: **Writing in paragraphs**

In the examination you will have to write an essay-style answer on Germany 1918–1945 in approximately 40 minutes. When producing an essay-style answer, it is important that you write in paragraphs. You will need to make a number of points to build up your argument so that it answers the question you have been asked. You should write a paragraph to address each point.

## What should you include in a paragraph?

In a paragraph you should:

- make a point to support your argument and answer the question
- provide evidence to support your point
- explain how your evidence supports your point
- explain how your point relates to the essay question.

**Remember: POINT — EVIDENCE — EXPLANATION**

It is important that you construct your answer in this way. If you just 'tell a story' in which you produce factual knowledge without explanation, you will not get high marks.

## An example

Here is an example of a question asking you to produce not a story, but an explanation:

(A) Why did Germany experience acute political and economic instability in the years 1919–1923?

The information to answer this question can be found in Section 1: The fall of the Second Reich. Here are some points you could include.

- International factors – the impact of the Treaty of Versailles and ongoing disputes over reparations.
- The right-wing factor – the new democratic republic was attacked by Germany's powerful conservative elites who wanted to discredit, weaken and destroy it.
- The Communist factor – the Weimar Republic was challenged from the left by Communists who wanted to see it replaced by a workers' state.
- Social factors – the underlying divisions in German society which gave rise to a multi-party political system and made it difficult to form stable governments.
- The economic policy of 1923 – a serious inflation problem originating in the decision to pay for the war with borrowed money.

As you plan, it is important to have a clear idea about the relative importance of the factors you are discussing. You should decide which factor is most important. Your answer should be clearly written and you should aim to convince the examiner that your opinion is correct.

Here is an example of a paragraph that could form part of your answer:

The activities of the extreme right were the main reason why Germany experienced acute political instability in the early 1920s. The conservative elites – the Junkers, the army officers and big businessmen – hated the Weimar Republic and used their power and influence to try to destroy it. They had the ability to influence public opinion through Alfred Hugenberg's media empire and they had at their disposal paramilitary organisations like the Stahlhelm. The most obvious way in which extreme right-wingers disrupted political life in Germany in the years up to 1923 was their use of force in the Kapp Putsch, the Organisation Consul murder campaign and the 'Beer Hall Putsch'. But they contributed to political instability in other ways as well. They created a tense and poisonous atmosphere in Germany by creating the 'stab-in-the-back' myth and by blaming Republican politicians for the Versailles 'Diktat' and the Ruhr occupation. Moderate politicians in the early 1920s believed that the extreme right was the most disruptive force at work in Germany and they were right.

This is a good paragraph because:

- It begins with a clear statement which identifies a reason for political instability in Germany in the early 1920s.
- It prioritises reasons by suggesting that the activities of the extreme right were the most important cause of political instability in Germany.

- The opening statement is backed up by evidence. The paragraph gives examples of who the extreme right were, how powerful they were and how they used their power.

- It explains how the point made in the paragraph relates to the question set.

## Activity: Spot the mistake

Below are three paragraphs which attempt to explain why the activities of the extreme right were the most important cause of political instability in Germany in the early 1920s. However, although the information in each paragraph is correct, there are mistakes in the way in which each paragraph is written. Your task is to spot the mistake and write one sentence of advice to the author of each paragraph explaining how he or she could do better.

## Example 1

When the Free Corps were given orders to disband in 1920, Ehrhardt was not prepared to accept them. Instead, in partnership with Luttwitz and Kapp, he seized control of Berlin and proclaimed the overthrow of the Weimar Republic. After his putsch failed, Ehrhardt turned to assassination as a means of attacking the Republic. He formed Organisation Consul, the murder gang which claimed the lives of Erzberger and Rathenau. There was a further extreme right-wing putsch attempt in 1923 after 'passive resistance' was called off. It can therefore be seen that the extreme right bore a lot of responsibility for political instability in Germany in the early 1920s.

## Example 2

The extreme right opposed the Weimar Republic for a variety of reasons. Extreme right-wingers resented the fact that they had lost the political influence to which they had become accustomed before 1918. They also had contempt for the Social Democratic founders of the Republic, believing them to be unpatriotic. Finally, they believed that Weimar politicians were responsible for Germany's defeat in the war, claiming that they

had agreed to an armistice when the German army was capable of fighting on.

## Example 3

Extreme right-wingers attacked the Weimar Republic throughout the 1920s. In the Republic's early years they thought in terms of overthrowing it by means of a putsch. The putsch attempts of 1920 and 1923 were serious threats to the stability of the Republic. In the later 1920s, though, other tactics were used to destabilise Weimar democracy. Hitler and the Nazis fought street battles against Communist paramilitaries with the intention of giving the impression that Germany was in a state of crisis.

**Answers**

Example 1 – describes some of the things the extreme right did, but does not answer the question.

Example 2 – misses the point of the question by focusing on why the extreme right hated the Weimar Republic as opposed to its importance as a cause of instability.

Example 3 – contains some material which could be made relevant but goes outside the specified period.

## Activity: Write your own paragraph

Here is an example of the style of question often used in the examination. It asks you to make a judgment about the relative importance of causes.

(B)  How accurate is it to suggest that the Treaty of Versailles was mainly responsible for the political and economic instability in Germany in the years 1919–1923?

If you were writing an essay-style answer to this question, you would be expected to select information which helps to explain why there was political and economic instability in Germany in 1919–1923 and to decide on the importance of the Treaty of Versailles and its impact compared to other factors, such as hostility to the Republic from the extreme right and extreme left and the social divisions which gave rise to multi-party politics. There may be other factors you may wish to add. Using the steps outlined above to help you, write a paragraph to form part of an essay in answer to the question.

# Chapter 5  The Nazi Party: origins, ideas, early development

---

### Key questions
- What developments took place within the Nazi Party in its earliest years?
- What did the Nazis stand for?
- How was the Nazi Party reorganised after the Munich *putsch*?

---

When the Weimar Republic was founded, Adolf Hitler was a 30-year-old soldier in the German army based in Munich. Up to this point his life had been lived in obscurity. Austrian-born, he had behind him an undistinguished school career, two rejected art school applications, five years living as a drop-out in pre-war Vienna and four years' service as a low-ranking soldier on the Western Front. The course of Hitler's life changed in 1919 when he was ordered by his superiors to look into a tiny political grouping called the German Workers' Party (DAP). Hitler duly attended DAP meetings and became active in its affairs. In the process he discovered that he was a gifted public speaker. By the time DAP renamed itself the National Socialist German Workers' Party (NSDAP) in 1920, Hitler was the dominant figure within it. At this point he left the army to devote himself to the NSDAP on a full-time basis. In the years that followed, Hitler made a name for himself in the limited world of Bavarian right-wing politics, but success at the national level proved more elusive. In 1929, after nearly ten years of campaigning, the NSDAP was still only a fringe player in German politics.

---

### Timeline

| | |
|---|---|
| **1920** | Foundation of the NSDAP;  publication of the NSDAP's Twenty-Five Point Programme |
| **1923** | The 'Beer Hall Putsch' took place in Munich |
| **1924** | Hitler's treason trial |
| **1925** | Publication of *Mein Kampf* ('My Struggle') |
| **1926** | Bamberg Conference |
| **1929** | Hitler and the Nazis invited to join Hugenberg's campaign against the Young Plan |

### Take note

Make a list of the main events in the growth of the NSDAP between 1920 and 1929. In relation to each event you identify, write two or three sentences explaining (i) its importance and (ii) whether what happened resulted from the actions of Hitler or the Nazis or from the actions of others.

## The NSDAP, 1920–1923

When Hitler first joined the DAP it was a political debating society rather than a fully-fledged political party. It had no programme, no headquarters and no organisational structure. Hitler's immediate aims after he became its leader were to give it a clear identity and to transform it into an organisation capable of waging political warfare. In the first two years of his leadership a significant amount of progress was made.

> ### Anton Drexler, DAP leader, speaking about Hitler in 1919
> 'Goodness, he's got a gob. We could use him.'

- A policy statement, the Twenty-Five Point Programme, was published in early 1920.

- The party began to call itself the National Socialist German Workers' Party (NSDAP).

- A newspaper, the *Volkischer Beobachter* ('People's Observer'), was bought to popularise the party's views.

- A network of local party branches was set up, most of them in Bavaria, with only a small number in other parts of Germany.

- Party rallies were held and were increasingly well attended.

- A paramilitary organisation, the SA or storm troop, was established in 1921.

By 1922 the NSDAP had around 6,000 members. This number increased sharply following the French occupation of the Ruhr and had reached 50,000 by the time of the ill-fated *putsch* attempt in Munich in November 1923 (see the section on Hitler's treason trial on page 39).

## What did the Nazis stand for?

Hitler was neither a systematic nor an original thinker. Nor did he have any real interest in ideas for their own sake. He despised intellectuals. He saw himself as an agitator, a propagandist and a man of action. His outlook meant that Nazism was not so much a carefully worked out, fully coherent political doctrine as a bundle of instincts, hatreds and prejudices. The **Nazis'** core beliefs were ultra-nationalism, racism, **authoritarianism**, anti-capitalism and anti-Communism.

> ### 'Nazi'
> The word 'Nazi' originated as a slang term used by the NSDAP's opponents. It was a shortened version of the party's full name, in the same way that 'Sozi' in 1920s Germany was shorthand for Social Democrat. Members of the NSDAP did not describe themselves as Nazis but called themselves National Socialists.

> ### Hitler on his political beliefs, 1928
> 'I am a German nationalist. That is to say I am true to my nation. All my thoughts and actions are dedicated to it. I am a socialist. I recognise no class or status group, but rather a community of people, tied by blood, united by language.'

### Take note
As you read this chapter, make notes on Hitler's main successes and failures as a party leader in the 1920s. Note down specific examples in each case.

### Take note
Using your own words, explain the meaning the Nazis attached to the following terms: *Lebensraum*, Aryan, Slav, *Führerprinzip*, legality strategy, *Gauleiter*.

### Glossary

#### Authoritarianism
A form of government in which rule is imposed on people without their consent. Authoritarian governments typically govern without respect for the law or human rights and are quick to resort to intimidation and force if challenged.

| Ultra-nationalism | The Nazis believed that the most important division within humankind was the division into nations and nationalities. They further believed that nations competed against each other for survival and greatness. The Nazis' overriding aim was German greatness. What this meant in practice was regaining the territory lost under the Treaty of Versailles, creating a Germany which would contain all Europe's German-speaking peoples within its borders and expanding to the east to carve out *Lebensraum* or 'living space' for Germans at the expense of the Soviet Union. The Nazis believed that an individual's duty to serve the nation was more important than any other obligation he or she had. |
|---|---|
| Racism and anti-Semitism | The Nazis were racists – that is, they believed that humankind was divided into biologically distinct groups, some of which were superior to others. They did not, however, distinguish sharply between races and nationalities. In Nazism the line between the two was blurred. At the top of the Nazis' racial hierarchy was the Aryan, or Nordic, 'master race' to which Germans belonged: at the bottom were the Slavs of eastern Europe and Russia, seen by the Nazis as 'sub-human'. The Nazis saw Europe's Jews as a separate race who, if left unchecked, would achieve world domination. |
| Authoritarianism | The Nazis maintained that if Germany was to succeed in the struggle between nations it had to be ruled in a pitiless fashion by an all-powerful leader. They rejected democracy completely. They believed that democracy encouraged conflict between different elements within the nation and so stood in the way of national unity and national revival.<br>A second reason for the Nazis' rejection of democracy was their contemptuous view of ordinary people. The masses, said Hitler, were 'blind and stupid'. |
| Anti-capitalism | Significant elements within the NSDAP were deeply hostile to big business. They were sympathetic to the plight of small businessmen and traders who they thought were being squeezed between the forces of trade unionism on the one hand and big business on the other. Hitler, though, never took the anti-capitalist dimension of Nazism seriously. He called himself a socialist when it suited him, but he defined the term in such a way as to deprive it of any real meaning. |

Nazi beliefs

### How did Nazi beliefs differ from those of the conservative elites?

There was a lot of common ground between the Nazis and the conservative elites. Both were ultra-nationalist. Both were anti-Communist, anti-Semitic and anti-democratic. But there were issues on which they were divided.

- The conservative elites wanted a restoration of the monarchy: the Nazis did not. Hitler wanted Germany to be ruled by what he called 'a man chosen by destiny to lead'.

- The conservative elites were old-fashioned imperialists who hoped to regain Germany's lost colonies. Hitler displayed little interest in overseas colonies. Instead he thought in terms of a 'drive to the east' to seize territory and resources from the Soviet Union.

- The conservative elites were suspicious of a movement which labelled its ideas 'National Socialism' and supported anti-capitalist proposals.

- The Nazis spoke of creating a new society, a 'National Community', which was not divided by class and status. This apparent belief in equality alarmed the conservative elites.

## Hitler's treason trial, 1924

In November 1923, soon after Stresemann started to bring Germany's hyperinflation nightmare to an end by calling off passive resistance, Hitler marched into a Munich beer hall where Gustav von Kahr, head of Bavaria's state government, was speaking. He forced von Kahr at gunpoint to agree to set in motion the right-wing march on Berlin they had both been involved in planning. Naively, Hitler then let von Kahr go. Von Kahr promptly ordered forces loyal to him to occupy key points around the city. When the Nazis took to the streets and advanced towards a barricade set up by von Kahr's forces, a 30-second shoot-out took place which left 18 people dead. Most of the 2,000 Nazi marchers fled.

These events led to Hitler being put on trial for treason in February–March 1924. At the trial, aided by a sympathetic judge, he ran rings round his prosecutors and turned the court-room into a platform for Nazi propaganda. He was found guilty but was given an absurdly light sentence of five years' imprisonment. In the event he was released on parole after less than a year in December 1924. He occupied himself in prison by writing **Mein Kampf**.

The treason trial was an important stage in the development of Nazism because it attracted a huge amount of publicity. It made Hitler a nationally known figure in Germany for the first time. There was a second reason why the trial was important. Before it, Hitler saw himself as someone who was helping to prepare the ground for a saviour who would rise up and restore Germany to greatness. After it, he believed himself to be that saviour.

## Hitler reasserts his authority

While Hitler was in prison the NSDAP fell into disarray. It was banned by law from campaigning; its leaders were scattered, with some in prison and others in exile; and factional squabbling broke out, in particular between Hitler's Munich-based cronies and the anti-capitalist north German wing of the party headed by **Gregor Strasser**.

Hitler's first task on his release from prison was to end the bickering within the NSDAP and to unify the party under his control. This he did at the Bamberg Conference in 1926. Sixty of the NSDAP's top leaders were subjected to a two-hour rant in which Hitler demanded unquestioning acceptance of his authority. Hitler also announced that there would be no changes to Nazi policy along the anti-capitalist lines favoured by Gregor Strasser. Strasser accepted this without protest. Hitler rewarded him by making him party propaganda chief.

In the later 1920s Hitler tightened his grip over the NSDAP by imposing the 'leadership principle' (*Führerprinzip*) on it. Individuals at each level of the party hierarchy were required to offer total and unhesitating obedience to their superiors. At the top of this military-style structure was the *Führer* (leader) who had dictatorial authority within the party and was accountable to no one. An indication of the increasingly leadership-centred nature of the NSDAP was the requirement on party members from 1926 onwards to use the Hitler salute ('*Heil Hitler!*') when greeting each other.

### Mein Kampf

*Mein Kampf* ('My Struggle') was a book which ran to more than 750 pages in its original form. A rambling, incoherent affair, it was in part an autobiography, in part a statement of Hitler's political beliefs and in part a guide to how to be a political agitator. However, it left no doubt about the centrality of anti-Communism, anti-Semitism and the need for German expansion eastwards in Hitler's thinking.

### Biography

### Gregor Strasser
(1892–1934)

In the 1920s Gregor Strasser was the NSDAP's most important leader after Hitler. Hitler was jealous of him: Strasser was highly educated; he had served in the trenches during the war as an officer; and after the war he became a successful businessman. Strasser's main aim in the mid-1920s was to persuade the NSDAP to adopt what he called 'German socialism' – in other words, his anti-capitalist programme. It was never his intention to take over as Nazi leader himself.

Gregor Strasser in 1932

**Hitler describing his new political strategy, 1924**

'Instead of working to achieve power by armed uprising, we shall have to hold our noses and enter the Reichstag against the Catholic and Communist members. Sooner or later we shall have a majority and after that we shall have Germany.'

## A new political strategy: 'legality'

While in prison Hitler reassessed the NSDAP's political strategy. He decided in the light of the events of November 1923 to abandon the *putsch* as a means of winning power. Instead he committed the NSDAP to a policy of so-called 'legality'. This involved contesting elections with the object of building up a base within the Reichstag from which a final assault on power could be made. The 'legality' strategy did not mean that the Nazis had renounced violence or that the paramilitaries of the SA were made redundant – nor did it mean that the Nazis now believed in parliamentary democracy. The SA, no longer required in its previous capacity as the NSDAP's battering ram in a *putsch*, was given a new role: to attack Communist paramilitaries on the streets of Germany's towns and cities. The idea was to weaken the Weimar Republic by giving the impression that it was incapable of maintaining law and order. 'Legality' was thus a twin-track strategy which involved the calculated use of violence as well as participation in the electoral process.

In the late 1920s Hitler ordered a major reorganisation of the NSDAP. The aim was to enhance its ability to fight election campaigns. Under the new arrangements the NSDAP was divided into 35 areas, or *Gaue*, with borders which corresponded to those of Weimar Germany's 35 electoral districts. Each area had its own leader, or *Gauleiter*, who was responsible for all political activity within it. The *Gauleiters* were directly accountable to Hitler. Included in their ranks were some of his most energetic subordinates, notably Josef Goebbels, *Gauleiter* of Berlin (see page 46).

## Conclusion: how strong was the Nazi political position in 1929?

**The Nazis' new election-based strategy did not bring immediate results. In the 1928 Reichstag elections they won less than 3 percent of the vote. The later 1920s, however, were not entirely barren years for the NSDAP. Between 1923 and 1929 party membership doubled from 50,000 to more than 100,000. This increase owed much to Hitler's political skills, among them his capacity to inspire loyalty and his remarkable prowess as a public speaker. In addition, the NSDAP received a boost in 1929 when Hugenberg, leader of the Nationalist Party, invited it to join his campaign against the arrangements for the payment of reparations set out in the Young Plan. This gave the Nazis a status and a respectability which they had not previously had. They had begun to edge in to the mainstream of German politics.**

## Activity: analysing Nazism in the 1920s

**Taking it further**

If you want to study further the divisions in the Nazi Party in the 1920s, read chapter 5 of Frank McDonough (2003) *Hitler and the Rise of the Nazi Party*. On the basis of this chapter and Documents 10-12 printed in the Documents section of the book, write a paragraph explaining how Hitler's views on socialism differed from those of Strasser and his followers.

- In what ways, and to what extent, were the Nazis a divided party in the 1920s?

- What arguments could be used to support the view that Nazism was an inconsistent and incoherent political doctrine?

- How significantly did the Nazis' political ideas differ from those of Germany's conservative elites?

# Chapter 6 **The Nazi electoral breakthrough, 1928–1932**

## Key questions

- What kinds of people became Nazi voters in and after 1930?
- Which sections of society were most resistant to the appeal of Nazism?
- What explanations can be given for the Nazi electoral breakthrough?

In the four years between 1928 and 1932 the number of Germans voting for the Nazis rose from 800,000 to nearly 14 million. This swift and spectacular electoral breakthrough has been extensively studied by historians: there cannot be many other events in 20th century European history which have been studied more. Historical research has centred on two closely related questions: what sort of people voted for the Nazis, and why did they do so? Owing to the nature of the available evidence, these have not proved to be easy questions to answer. There were no public opinion polls in pre-1933 Germany to discover what motivated people to vote for one party rather than another. Quite a lot of individuals have left behind evidence about their voting behaviour in diaries and reminiscences, but this kind of evidence presents the problem of deciding how typical or representative the people who produced it were. The main source of evidence which historians are left with is election statistics from the period 1918–1933. These statistics have been examined from different viewpoints. Looking at trends in support for different parties over time has allowed conclusions to be drawn about what kinds of people made the switch to Nazism and what kinds did not. Even more informative has been the study of the geography of German elections: historians have looked at patterns of voting in different regions and localities and have cross-referenced these patterns with what is known about the social and economic make-up of these regions and localities. Much is now known for certain about who voted Nazi and why, but some areas of uncertainty and controversy remain.

| Timeline: Elections in Germany, 1928–1933 | |
|---|---|
| **1928** | Reichstag election: Nazis won 0.8 million votes and 12 seats |
| **1930** | Reichstag election: Nazis won 6.4 million votes and 107 seats |
| **1932 (Mar–Apr)** | Presidential election: Hitler won 11.3 million votes in the first round and 13.4 million in the second round |
| **1932 (Jul)** | Reichstag election: Nazis won 13.8 million votes and 230 seats |
| **1932 (Nov)** | Reichstag election: Nazis won 11.7 million votes and 196 seats |
| **1933 (Mar)** | Reichstag election: Nazis won 17.3 million votes and 288 seats (Note: this election took place after considerable Nazi intimidation and the banning of the German Communist Party) |

**Take note**

As you read through this chapter, construct a diagram – either a mind map or a table – showing (i) what kinds of people became Nazi voters after 1930, and (ii) the reasons why they were attracted to the Nazi Party.

## Political parties in the Weimar era

It is impossible to understand the Nazis' electoral breakthrough without an awareness of the political context in which it was made. This involves taking a look at the party system of the Weimar Republic.

The Weimar party system had two key characteristics.

- It was a multi-party system. There were five or six major political parties in Weimar Germany capable of winning 10 percent or more of the vote in national elections. Conversely, there was no single party capable of winning anywhere near 50 percent of the vote in national elections. This is why there were no single-party governments in the Weimar era. Weimar governments were coalitions made up of three or four different political parties. This in turn helps to explain why in the 11 years between 1919 and 1930 no fewer than 16 separate governments held office in Germany.

- The political parties of the Weimar era were 'sectional' parties in that they represented the interests of particular sections of the community – workers, Catholics, professional people, Junkers and so on. They attracted little or no support from outside their own 'camp'. There were no real national parties in the Weimar Republic – that is, political parties which attracted support from different sections of the community and whose appeal cut across the boundaries of class and religion.

| WORKING-CLASS CAMP | | CATHOLIC CAMP | MIDDLE-CLASS CAMP | | CONSERVATIVE CAMP |
|---|---|---|---|---|---|
| **Communist Party (KPD)** | **Social Democratic Party (SPD)** | **Centre Party (*Zentrum*)** | **Democratic Party (DDP)** | **People's Party (DVP)** | **Nationalist Party (DNVP)** |
| Younger and less-skilled workers; unemployed workers | Older and more skilled workers The party of the majority of the working class | Catholics of all social classes – aristocrats, middle class and workers | Intellectuals and professional people: sometimes called 'the professors' party' | Industrialists, businessmen, managers Stresemann's party | Junkers and industrial tycoons Hugenberg's party |

Weimar political parties and their support

## Who voted Nazi?

A study of the performance of the main political parties in Reichstag elections between 1919 and 1933 (see table below) offers clear pointers to the identity of the kinds of voter who turned to the Nazis after 1930. Support for the Centre Party was broadly stable throughout the Weimar era, suggesting that Catholics for the most part were resistant to the appeal of Nazism. The Social Democratic Party's vote was more erratic than the Centre Party's, but it retained much of its hold on the working-class vote during the period of the Nazi breakthrough. This suggests that the Nazis failed to win over the majority of working-class voters. On the other hand, support for the established middle-class parties (DDP and DVP) collapsed in the early 1930s.

This suggests that middle-class voters switched to the Nazis in droves. The decline in support for the Nationalist Party in the early 1930s suggests that large parts of the conservative camp followed suit.

| Party | 1919 | 1920 | 1924 (May) | 1924 (Dec) | 1928 | 1930 | 1932 (July) | 1932 (Dec) | 1933 |
|---|---|---|---|---|---|---|---|---|---|
| KPD | – | 2% | 12% | 9% | 11% | 13% | 14% | 17% | 12% |
| SPD | 38% | 21% | 21% | 26% | 30% | 24% | 22% | 20% | 19% |
| Centre (Zentrum) | 20% | 18% | 17% | 18% | 15% | 15% | 16% | 15% | 14% |
| Democratic Party (DDP) | 19% | 8% | 6% | 6% | 5% | 4% | 1% | 1% | 1% |
| People's Party (DVP) | 4% | 14% | 9% | 10% | 9% | 5% | 1% | 2% | 1% |
| Nationalists (DNVP) | 10% | 15% | 19% | 21% | 14% | 7% | 6% | 9% | 8% |
| Nazis (NSDAP) | – | – | 7% | 3% | 2% | 18% | 37% | 33% | 44% |
| Others | 9% | 22% | 8% | 7% | 14% | 14% | 3% | 3% | 1% |

Reichstag elections 1919–1933 (% share of the vote won by major parties)

> **Take note**
>
> What changes took place in the early 1930s in the voting behaviour of (i) the working-class camp, (ii) the middle-class camp and (iii) the conservative camp?

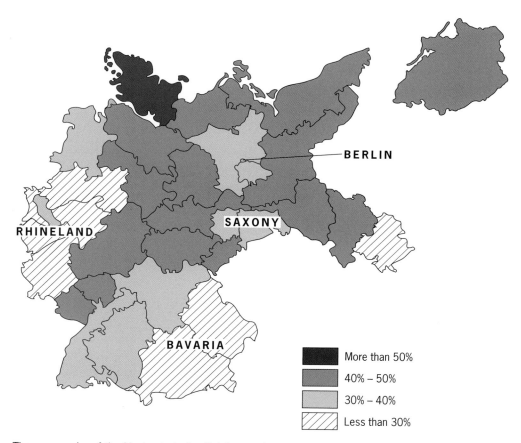

The geography of the Nazi vote in the Reichstag election of July 1932

Legend:
- More than 50%
- 40% – 50%
- 30% – 40%
- Less than 30%

A study of electoral geography at the regional level points in the same direction as a study of electoral trends over time: support for the Nazis during their breakthrough period was weaker in Catholic areas (such as Bavaria and the Rhineland) and industrial areas (such as Berlin and Saxony) than it was elsewhere.

It is instructive to look at voting patterns in particular neighbourhoods as well as in whole regions. If the focus is narrowed in this way, what becomes clear is that the Nazis had quite a lot of success in winning over working-class voters. Even in the most deprived working-class districts of Berlin such as Neukölln and Wedding around one-fifth of voters were supporting the Nazis by 1932 (see table). The majority of the working-class camp remained loyal to either the SPD or KPD, but a significant minority within it did not. This enabled the Nazis to claim that they drew their support from all sections of the community. Unlike all other Weimar political parties, they were, so they said, a 'people's party' – a party which represented the whole of the German nation.

| Neighbourhood | 1928 election | 1930 election | July 1932 election |
|---|---|---|---|
| Wilmersdorf (upper middle-class suburb) | 2% | 19% | 35% |
| Zehlendorf (upper middle-class suburb) | 2% | 18% | 37% |
| Wedding (deprived working-class district) | 1% | 9% | 19% |
| Neukölln (deprived working-class district) | 1% | 11% | 24% |

Nazi share of the vote in four Berlin neighbourhoods, 1928–1932

What is known about who voted Nazi after 1930 and who did not can be summed up as follows:

- Catholics were less likely to vote Nazi than Protestants.

- Support for the Nazis was strong among middle- and upper-class voters.

- The Nazis attracted a large following in the small towns and rural areas of Protestant northern Germany.

- The Nazis had fewer supporters among the working class than they did among the middle classes, but by 1932 they had won over a significant minority of the working class.

- Gender does not appear to have been a factor in determining whether someone voted Nazi or not: men and women voted for and against the Nazis in roughly the same proportions.

- Whether or not age was an influence on voting Nazi is a matter of controversy: some historians argue that younger voters were especially strongly attracted to the Nazis but others insist this was not the case.

# Why did people vote Nazi?

The Nazis' electoral prospects were transformed above all else by the world economic depression which began with the Wall Street Crash in 1929. Germany's economy was heavily dependent on loans from the USA and as a result it was hit harder by the economic slump than any other European country. Its banking system was plunged into crisis as foreign investors hurried to withdraw their money. Unemployment increased from approximately 1.5 million in 1929 to 3 million in 1930 before reaching over 6 million in 1932. Nor were those who kept their jobs unaffected: they were hit by severe **deflation**, which saw wages and prices falling sharply.

## Middle-class voters

There are a variety of possible reasons why middle-class voters, already disillusioned with the Weimar Republic, turned to the Nazis in this crisis. Some may have been attracted to them as a new party untainted by involvement in the Republic's failures; others may have been impressed by Hitler's apparent drive and charisma; and hard-hit small businessmen may have believed the Nazis would protect them from ruin. But probably the most important reason why middle-class voters were drawn to Nazism was fear of Communism. Between 1928 and 1932 the number of people voting for the KPD increased from 3 million to 5 million. In addition, the paramilitaries of the Red Front Fighters' League were an ever-more visible presence on the streets of Germany's major cities. To the middle classes the possibility of a Communist take-over in Germany seemed real. It was a prospect which reduced them to a state of near-panic. The attraction of the Nazis in these circumstances was that far more than anyone else they appeared to have the strength and determination to take on the KPD and destroy it. The Nazis' reputation for brutality had previously alienated the respectable middle classes but it now became an asset.

## Working-class voters

Explaining why members of the working class voted Nazi is not easy. There were German workers who were conservatives and nationalists – just as there were working-class conservatives in Britain – and they may have been stirred by Nazi promises of national revival. Other workers may have been impressed by the Nazi vow to provide 'work and bread'. Many of the workers who turned to the Nazis, though, seem to have been people who had the same kind of fears as the middle classes. Typically, they were self-employed workers such as carpenters, plumbers and housepainters rather than factory workers – that is, they were people who stood outside the highly organised and close-knit sub-cultures associated with the Social Democratic and Communist parties. Badly hit by the economic slump and fearing disorder, they may have felt the Nazis offered the best hope of a return to some sort of stability.

## Glossary

### Deflation

The opposite of inflation: inflation means rising prices, deflation means falling prices. Deflation occurs when demand for goods and services plummets, forcing producers and traders to cut wages and prices in order to stay in business. In 1932 wages and prices in Germany were about 30 percent lower than they had been in 1929. It is important to understand that the economic problems facing Germany after 1929 were very different from those experienced in 1923.

### Otto Strasser on Hitler's impact as a public speaker, 1940

'Adolf Hitler enters a hall. He sniffs the air. For a minute he gropes, feels his way, senses the atmosphere. Suddenly he bursts forth. His words go like an arrow to their target. He touches each wound on the raw, liberating the mass unconscious, expressing its innermost terrors, telling it what it most wants to hear.'

## Biography

### Josef Goebbels
(1897–1945)

The master propagandist of Nazism. Born into a lower middle-class Catholic family in western Germany, Goebbels excelled at school and received a doctorate in literature from one of Germany's most prestigious universities. He was drawn into Nazi politics after a hoped-for literary career failed to get off the ground. Initially he was a disciple of Gregor Strasser, but after the 1926 Bamberg Conference became one of Hitler's most devoted followers. Hitler posted him to Berlin as *Gauleiter* in 1926 and in 1933 he was appointed Minister of Propaganda and National Enlightenment. His academic qualifications and physical disability – a damaged foot, the legacy of childhood polio – made him the target of unflattering gossip in the rough, male-dominated world of Nazi politics. His response was to make sure that no one outdid him when it came to being brutal and abrasive. Goebbels was among the most poisonous of all the Nazi leaders.

Industrial workers who had lived out their lives under the Communist or Social Democratic umbrellas do not appear to have voted Nazi in large numbers. They were strongly attached to the 'camp', or sub-culture, of which they felt themselves to be a part, and this was reflected in the way they voted. The reluctance of Catholic voters to give up on the Centre Party can be explained in the same way.

## Nazi propaganda

In political terms the Nazis clearly benefited enormously from the post-1929 economic slump. Before it they were a fringe party: after it they were not. It would, however, be wrong to think that votes simply fell into their lap without much effort on their part to win them. The fact is that the Nazis exploited the opportunity they were given after 1929 with energy, skill and flair. When it came to **propaganda** they were far superior to any of Germany's other political parties.

In the early 1930s the Nazis campaigned harder than any of their rivals. They held more meetings and produced more leaflets and posters than the other parties. They also campaigned more imaginatively than others – making use, for example, of the medium of film to get their message across to the voters. Much of the imagination in Nazi campaigning was supplied by **Josef Goebbels**, the party's propaganda chief from 1930 onwards.

- One of the Nazis' trump cards in propaganda terms was Hitler's charismatic personality. This found expression in his public speeches. It appears that many who heard him speak in this period were spellbound and went away convinced that he was dynamic, decisive and sincere in his desire to create a new Germany. (See previous page, Strasser.)

- A particularly effective Nazi propaganda tactic involved targeting different groups in society and making separate, distinctive, tailor-made appeals to each of them. In the words of the German historian Bernd Weisbrod, the Nazis 'spoke in many tongues and promised almost anything to everybody'. An example of this tactic is the way in which the Nazis wooed Germany's farmers. In the early 1930s German farmers had three main grievances: low farm prices, for which foreign competition was largely responsible; debt, incurred because farmers preferred borrowing heavily to leaving the land; and the feeling that Weimar politicians were indifferent to their plight. The Nazis made farmers a series of promises: to introduce tariffs to protect them against foreign competition; to deal with the Jewish financiers who they claimed were responsible for the farmers' debt problems; and to give farmers an honoured place at the heart of the 'National Community'. This message was disseminated in rural areas by a purpose-built Nazi propaganda unit known as the Agricultural Apparatus. Other groups were targeted in similar fashion: the young, women, factory workers, civil servants and so on. By using this tactic, the Nazis turned themselves into what one historian (Childers, 1983) calls 'a catch-all party of protest' and another (Evans, 2004) calls 'a rainbow coalition of the discontented'.

At the same time that they were bombarding different social groups with specially tailored messages, the Nazis were also claiming to be the only party in Germany whose aim was to further the interests of the nation as a whole as opposed to the interests of sections of it. Once in power, they declared, they would create a National Community (*Volksgemeinschaft*) in which people of different groups and classes would work harmoniously together for the good of the country.

## Conclusion: how spectacular was the Nazi electoral breakthrough?

After 1929 there was a mass of insecurity and fear around in Germany for right-wing extremists to exploit. They were helped too by the fact that confidence in democratic government was in sharp decline. The Nazis were therefore operating in conditions which from their point of view were highly favourable. The same, of course, was true of other right-wing extremists, notably Hugenberg's Nationalists. Yet these others failed where the Nazis succeeded. Conservative elite politicians proved no match for the Nazis when it came to fighting election campaigns. As propagandists the Nazis reigned supreme. Their electoral achievement, however, had its limits. The Nazis never got close in a free election to winning the support of a majority of German voters. Nor could the continued loyalty of their new voters be taken for granted. In 1930 a German political commentator, Helmuth Gerlach, maintained that Nazi support was a mile wide but only an inch deep. 'If the sun shines once more on the German economy', he added, 'Hitler's voters will melt away like snow.'

## Activity: debating the Nazi electoral breakthrough

- Listed below are five reasons for the Nazis' electoral breakthrough. Select the one you think is (i) most important, and (ii) least important, giving reasons for your choice.

  *Middle-class fears of Communism.*
  *The targeting of the agricultural vote.*
  *The Nazi promise to create a 'National Community'.*
  *The Nazi promise to provide 'work and bread' for the unemployed.*
  *Hitler's impact as a public speaker.*

- In his speeches in the 1920s Hitler repeatedly claimed that (i) Germany's Jews were responsible for the country's misfortunes, and (ii) the difficulties Germany experienced after 1919 owed much to the Versailles *Diktat*. In light of the information in this chapter, do you think that the Nazis' anti-Semitism and their attacks on the Treaty of Versailles were important factors in their electoral breakthrough?

- The Nazis appealed to different voters in different ways. What sort of message do you think the Nazis would have sent to the following groups of people in order to gain their support: big business; skilled workers; farmers; industrial workers; Catholics; Nationalists?

### Hitler, speaking about the need for *Volksgemeinschaft*, 1932

'The workers have their own parties. The middle class needs even more parties. And the Catholics too, they have their own party. Thirty parties in one little land. And this at a time when before us lie the greatest tasks, which can only be undertaken if the strength of the whole nation is put together. Our enemies accuse us National Socialists of intolerance. They are right. We are intolerant. I have given myself one aim: to sweep the thirty parties out of Germany.'

### Taking it further

If you want to find out more about who voted Nazi and why, a good starting point is Dick Geary, 'Who Voted for the Nazis?' in *History Today* (October 1998). Alternatively, look at Chapter 2 of the same author's *Hitler and Nazism* (2000).

# Chapter 7 Hitler's legal path to power, 1930–1933

## Key questions

- Why did 'presidential government' replace 'parliamentary government' in 1930?
- Why did the two versions of 'presidential government' attempted in 1930–1932 both fail?
- How, in early 1933, did Hitler turn limited power into absolute power?
- How did other political parties help Hitler into power?
- Did Hitler come to power legally?

Hitler made no secret of his contempt for the Weimar constitution. But he did not flagrantly disregard its rules in his pursuit of power. The appearance of winning power lawfully mattered to him: he did not want his enemies to be able to question the right of a Nazi government to rule. In a parliamentary system of government the normal route to power is to win a majority in parliament. But Hitler was not able to take this route: the Nazis' best result in a Reichstag election was the 44 percent share of the vote they won – following massive intimidation of their opponents – in 1933. This left them short of the majority they needed to control the Reichstag and form a government on their own. It also left them a long way short of the two-thirds majority in the Reichstag which was required to suspend or alter the Weimar constitution.

Yet in 1933, despite his lack of a parliamentary majority, Hitler overthrew the Weimar Republic without having to resort to armed force. After a fashion, he won power legally. He was able to do so for two main reasons. The first is that in 1930 changes took place in the way in which Germany was governed which presented the Nazis with an opportunity to achieve power through the back door. The second is that in the early 1930s the Nazis found people who were willing to collaborate with them, mostly from within Germany's conservative elites: Hitler was helped into power.

## Why did parliamentary government break down in 1930?

The constitution-makers of 1919 expected Germany to be governed in all but the most exceptional circumstances in much the same way as Britain: governments would remain in office between elections as long as they could count on the support of a majority in parliament, and they would use their majority in parliament to change the law in whatever ways they thought advisable. Between 1919 and 1930 these were the lines along which Germany was governed. But in 1930 two developments made parliamentary government of this kind impossible.

## Disagreement between the moderate parties

In 1930 Germany's government was a coalition made up of the four political parties which either favoured or accepted the democratic system: the Social Democrats, the Centre, the Democratic Party and the People's Party. The government was headed by a Social Democrat, Hermann Müller.

When unemployment began to rise, the three non-socialist parties in Müller's coalition called for cuts in government spending, in particular cuts in unemployment benefit. Their demand reflected mainstream economic thought at the time, which maintained that the best thing governments could do in an economic downturn was to cut expenditure, avoid borrowing and rely on the private sector to get the economy moving again. The Social Democrats, however, were unwilling to accept spending cuts. It was working-class Germans who would bear the brunt of any reduction in unemployment benefits, and the Social Democrats were unwilling to betray their own supporters. Müller's coalition, hopelessly deadlocked, broke up. No new government which commanded a majority in the Reichstag could be formed to replace it: the Social Democrats and the moderate non-socialist parties had fallen out; neither had enough votes in the Reichstag to form a government on its own; and the extremist parties of left and right stood gloating on the sidelines, relishing the failure of the parliamentary system.

## The 1930 Reichstag elections

The Reichstag elections later in 1930 made things worse. The moderate parties lost ground while the Nazis on the right and the Communists on the left made gains. The four democratic parties now had fewer than half the seats in the Reichstag between them. This meant that even if they had been able to overcome their differences they would not have been able to form a government which had a majority in the Reichstag.

| KPD | SPD | DDP | CENTRE | DVP | DNVP | NAZIS |
|-----|-----|-----|--------|-----|------|-------|
| 13% | 24% | 4% | 15% | 5% | 7% | 18% |

The position in the Reichstag after the 1930 election

Anti-democratic parties which refused to help make parliamentary government work

Party supporting parliamentary government but opposed to spending cuts

Parties supporting parliamentary government which wanted spending cuts

NOTE: 14% of seats in the Reichstag were held by other, minor parties

# What did 'presidential government' involve?

The collapse of parliamentary government in 1930 brought Article 48 of the Weimar constitution into play. This gave the President at times of national emergency the power to rule by issuing decrees which had the force of law. The constitution-makers of 1919 assumed that emergencies requiring the use of Article 48 would be rare. They also thought that such emergencies would be brief – a matter of days or weeks. They certainly did not foresee Germany being governed under Article 48 for years on end. But this is what now happened. 'Presidential government', as it became known, was technically lawful but no one had ever imagined that Germany would be ruled in this way.

## Biography

### Kurt von Schleicher
(1882–1934)

Schleicher was an army general. He headed the army unit which had responsibility for relations with politicians and the government. He was, in effect, the army's political spokesman. It was Schleicher's military connections which led Hindenburg to attach so much weight to his advice and guidance. Schleicher had a number of positive qualities, notably shrewdness and imagination, but he was also over-ambitious, manipulative and untrustworthy. He saw in the economic crisis an opportunity to do away with the parliamentary system – and to further his own career.

Kurt von Schleicher in 1932

### Take note

Make a list of Brüning's strengths and weaknesses as Chancellor.

'Presidential government' brought Hindenburg to the fore. He was now 83 years old and not in good health. He relied heavily on the circle of advisers he assembled around him. Most of these advisers were, like Hindenburg himself, extreme right-wingers and convinced opponents of democracy. 'Presidential government' meant that Germany's conservative elites were firmly back in the saddle. The most influential member of Hindenburg's circle of advisers was **Kurt von Schleicher**.

'Presidential government' did not involve the aged Hindenburg taking over everything personally and immersing himself in the detailed work of running the country. Germany continued to be governed on a day-to-day basis by a Chancellor and a group of ministers. But Chancellors could only implement their policies if Hindenburg was willing to use Article 48 to issue the necessary decrees on their behalf. Under 'presidential government' Chancellors were really no more than servants of the President. Hindenburg and his circle of advisers appointed Chancellors and could dismiss them. Chancellors no longer relied on the support of the Reichstag to implement their policies and were therefore no longer accountable to it. Now the Chancellor was accountable only to the President.

## Brüning's appointment as Chancellor, 1930

In 1930 Hindenburg, acting on Schleicher's recommendation, appointed as Chancellor a scholarly but dour and colourless financial expert, **Heinrich Brüning** of the Centre Party. Brüning was chosen for a number of reasons.

- He had served as an infantry officer on the Western Front between 1915 and 1918 and had been decorated for bravery. In the eyes of Hindenburg and the military men in his circle this was evidence of soundness and reliability.

- Brüning's political outlook was conservative. He had disapproved of the 1918–1919 revolution and privately hoped for the return of the monarchy.

- It was believed that Brüning's background in economics and finance meant that he was well qualified to tackle the problem of rising unemployment.

- It was within the Reichstag's power to obstruct 'presidential government'. The constitution gave it the right to overturn presidential decrees. Hindenburg's advisers hoped that Brüning's appointment would help to prevent difficulties of this kind because he was well known in the Reichstag, having been a member of it since 1924. Their hopes were not misplaced: in 1930 the Social Democrats, the largest party in the Reichstag, decided not to make life difficult for Brüning. They called their policy one of 'toleration'.

## Brüning's policies as Chancellor

- Brüning was a firm believer in the orthodox, mainstream economic ideas of his time. He assumed that the economy would eventually recover of its own accord. He saw the role of the government as helping things along by living strictly within its means, spending only what it could afford and not running up debts. In practice this meant deep cuts in government spending. Brüning reduced unemployment benefit and cut jobs and wages in the public sector. He even cut the pensions of disabled war veterans.

- There were exceptions to this policy of cost-cutting. Spending on the army was not cut and nor were there cuts in the subsidies paid to farmers in eastern Germany, many of them Junkers. Cuts in these two areas would not have been acceptable to Hindenburg and his advisers.

- Brüning was convinced that the German economy was massively weighed down by the need to pay reparations. He worked hard and successfully to rid it of this burden. Reparations payments were suspended by international agreement in 1931 and scrapped altogether in 1932. However, contrary to Brüning's expectations, these agreements did nothing at all to speed up Germany's economic recovery.

- Brüning's policies were deeply unpopular in Germany. They earned him the nickname of 'the Hunger Chancellor'. By 1932 it was clear that they were unsuccessful as well as unpopular. Unemployment was still rising. There was no real evidence to suggest that the end of the economic depression was in sight. Brüning's days as Chancellor were numbered.

## Why did Brüning lose office?

The main thing that cost Brüning his job was the failure of his economic policies. As the economy deteriorated, support for the Communists grew. Violent clashes between Communist and Nazi paramilitaries became increasingly frequent (see table). Middle-class fears of a Communist takeover intensified. In these circumstances, Schleicher, Hindenburg's most influential adviser, began in 1932 to think in terms of solutions to Germany's problems which did not involve Brüning.

| | **Communists** | **Nazis** | **Total** |
|---|---|---|---|
| 1930 | 44 | 17 | 61 |
| 1931 | 52 | 42 | 94 |
| 1932 | 75 | 84 | 159 |

Nazis and Communists killed in street fighting, 1930–1932

Two further developments in 1932 sealed Brüning's fate. First, relations between Hindenburg and Brüning turned sour. The two fell out over the shambles which occurred when Hindenburg's seven-year term as President expired in early 1932. Initially, Hindenburg hoped to avoid an election, expecting Brüning to persuade the Reichstag to vote to extend his term in office. Brüning tried to do so, but failed – leaving Hindenburg angry and frustrated. Then things got worse.

**Take note**

What were the differences between the first version of 'presidential government' which operated between 1930 and 1932 and the second version which began with von Papen's appointment as Chancellor?

**Biography**

### Heinrich Brüning (1885-1970)

A trained economist, Brüning belonged to the conservative wing of the Centre Party. He served as a member of the Reichstag between 1924 and 1933, and at the time of his appointment as Chancellor in 1930 was chairman of the Centre Party's group of representatives in the Reichstag. After Hitler came to power, Brüning left Germany for the United States, where he became a university professor.

Heinrich Brüning in 1930

### Take note

Explain why Hindenburg dismissed (i) Brüning, (ii) von Papen and (iii) Schleicher.

### Biography

#### Franz von Papen
(1879–1969)

Von Papen came from an impoverished Catholic aristocratic family but prospered through his marriage to the daughter of a wealthy industrialist. His career before 1932 was colourful but undistinguished. As a junior army officer in the First World War he was attached to the German embassy in Washington, but was expelled from the USA for spying. He subsequently saw action on the Western Front. Between 1921 and 1932 he was a member of the Prussian state parliament. In 1932 Britain's ambassador to Germany described him privately as 'a man of second-rate ability – a lightweight'.

Franz von Papen in 1933

Hitler decided to stand against Hindenburg in the presidential election which now had to take place. This meant a head-to-head contest between the two of them for the right-wing vote which Hindenburg saw as his own. To Hindenburg's acute embarrassment, Hitler did well enough in the election to deprive him of an overall majority – an outcome which necessitated a second, run-off election between the leading candidates. In the run-off election, Hindenburg defeated Hitler by 19 million votes to 13 million, but it was Hitler who won the right-wing vote. Hindenburg, to his fury, was re-elected largely on the basis of votes cast by people he disliked and distrusted – Catholics and Social Democrats.

Second, it became known in Junker circles that Brüning was toying with the idea of buying up insolvent Junker estates and settling unemployed workers on them. Outraged Junkers complained to Hindenburg that Brüning was an 'agrarian Bolshevik' – in other words, a wild extremist intent on seizing their property. Brüning was dismissed soon afterwards.

## Von Papen as Chancellor

The new Chancellor, **Franz von Papen**, was recommended to Hindenburg by Schleicher, just as Brüning had been. Von Papen's appointment was greeted in Germany with astonishment: he was a little-known figure with hard-line right-wing views and no experience of government. But his appointment made sense in the context of Schleicher's wider plans. Schleicher had reached the conclusion that Germany's deepening crisis called for the introduction of a more-extreme form of 'presidential government' than the one which had operated over the previous two years. He now wanted Germany to be run as a near-dictatorship by the President and the army, with the Reichstag being permanently sidelined. In order to bring this plan to fruition, Schleicher wanted to enlist the support of the Nazis: their involvement, given their popularity with the electorate, would provide the appearance of mass support for the idea of authoritarian rule. This is where von Papen came in: he was so right-wing that Hitler, or so it was thought, would be amenable to the idea of working with him.

Von Papen's appointment as Chancellor was not the only ploy Schleicher used to try to draw Hitler into his plans. A number of other steps were taken in mid-1932 which were designed to win over the Nazis.

- Ministers were appointed to serve alongside von Papen who were as right-wing as he was: the new government was quickly labelled 'the cabinet of barons'.

- The ban that Brüning had imposed on the SA was lifted.

- Von Papen's government called for new Reichstag elections, knowing that the Nazis were certain to do well in them.

- In flagrant violation of the constitution, von Papen removed the Social Democrat-controlled state government of Prussia from office. Hitler was glad because it had been a determined opponent of Nazism.

# Political intrigues, 1932–1933

In the election of July 1932 the Nazis won nearly 38 percent of votes cast and became the largest single party in the Reichstag. The election was the starting-point of a sixth-month period of intrigue and jockeying for position at the top of German politics which culminated with Hitler's appointment as Chancellor in January 1933.

After the July election an intensive round of talks took place involving Hitler, Schleicher, von Papen and Hindenburg. There was only one item on the agenda: the terms on which Hitler might join the government. Hitler made it clear he would not accept a supporting role: he insisted on being made Chancellor. Hindenburg – a snob who disliked Hitler on account of his lowly social origins – was unwilling to agree. At a key meeting in mid-August 1932 he sent Hitler packing.

Hitler and Hindenberg in 1933

> ### A statement published by Hindenburg's office after the August 1932 meeting with Hitler
>
> 'The President asked Herr Hitler whether he was prepared to enter the Government under the Chancellorship of Herr von Papen. Herr Hitler replied in the negative, and demanded that the President should confer upon him the leadership of the Government together with entire and complete control of the State. President von Hindenburg emphatically declined to accede to this request.'

**Take note**

As you read through this section, draw a timeline of the key events in Hitler's rise to power. Make brief notes on the consequences of each event.

The fall-out from the August meeting was extensive but complicated.

- Hitler, angry at being snubbed, took his revenge by ordering Nazi members of the Reichstag to join other political parties, including the Communists, in passing a vote of no-confidence in von Papen's government. This meant another Reichstag election. When it took place in November 1932, the Nazis suffered a reverse: two million fewer people voted for them than had done in the July election. Most of the deserters were right-wing voters annoyed by what they saw as Hitler's selfish refusal to work under von Papen. Some newspapers asked if the Nazi bubble had burst.

- Schleicher thought that von Papen – 'little Franz', as he called him behind his back – had now served his purpose and wanted rid of him. Hindenburg, though, had developed a strong personal attachment to von Papen and was reluctant to part with him. He only gave way when Schleicher told him that the army wanted von Papen out.

- In December 1932 Schleicher took over as Chancellor himself. His position, however, was precarious: he was short of political allies and had no real backing in the country at large. What he came up with was a hastily-improvised scheme to win support for his chancellorship which involved trying to persuade the 'socialist' wing of the NSDAP and SPD trade unionists to join forces behind a push to bring down unemployment. He even offered Gregor Strasser the Vice-Chancellorship. But Schleicher's plan was half-baked. It was fanciful to assume that the 'socialist' wing of the NSDAP could be easily prised away from the main body of the party. In addition, law-abiding Social Democrats and violent 'left-wing' Nazis had virtually nothing in common. Schleicher's plan came to nothing.

## The Nazis take power

### Hitler becomes Chancellor, January 1933

In January 1933 von Papen met Hitler in secret on five occasions. Out of these talks came an agreement under which Hitler was to become Chancellor and von Papen Vice-Chancellor. Von Papen then persuaded Hindenburg to agree to this proposal. An arrangement along these lines had proved impossible back in August 1932. Now the circumstances were different: Hitler, Hindenburg and von Papen were readier to compromise than they had been previously (see table below). Once the agreement was in place Hindenburg forced Schleicher out of office.

| | |
|---|---|
| **Hitler** | • He was under pressure from his own supporters to do a deal because after the November election there were worries that the Nazis were running out of steam and might not get into power.<br>• He wanted to punish Schleicher for offering the Vice-Chancellorship to Gregor Strasser – an offer which he saw as a deliberate attempt to split and destroy the Nazi movement. |
| **Hindenburg** | • He wanted his close friend von Papen back alongside him in government.<br>• He believed von Papen's assurances that Hitler could be controlled. |
| **Von Papen** | • He was deeply ambitious and was desperate to return to government – even if he did not get the top job.<br>• He was confident that he could control and manipulate Hitler: he told friends in January that he had 'hired' Hitler and would soon have him 'pushed into a corner'.<br>• He was bitter about the way Schleicher had engineered his dismissal as Chancellor in November 1932 and wanted his revenge. |

Hindenburg, Hitler and von Papen in January 1933: motives behind their agreement

Hitler did not win the absolute power he craved in January 1933. The government he led was a coalition in which only three out of twelve ministers were Nazis. More important, he was an Article 48 Chancellor who was reliant on Hindenburg in the same way Brüning, von Papen and Schleicher had been before him. Hitler's priority was to end 'presidential government' and to concentrate power in his own hands without acting unconstitutionally. This meant a further Reichstag election. A majority for the Nazis would mean they could make laws on their own, by-passing Hindenburg. A two-thirds majority would mean they could amend the Weimar constitution however they wished.

### The March 1933 election

The Nazis did everything in their power to win the 1933 election short of resorting to outright fraud. Opposition meetings were broken up; individuals were attacked and beaten by SA men who had been enrolled as volunteer policemen for the duration of the election campaign; and opposition newspapers were banned. There was a final dramatic twist to the election campaign in the shape of an arson attack on the Reichstag building, allegedly by a Dutch Communist, Marinus van der Lubbe. The **Reichstag Fire** was a godsend to the Nazis. It enabled them to play on middle-class fears of Communism by claiming that a Communist uprising was imminent. They also used the fire as a pretext to persuade Hindenburg to issue a decree suspending basic rights, such as freedom of speech and freedom of assembly. This decree – formally known as the Decree for the Protection of the People and the State, but often referred to as the Reichstag Fire decree – was then used to outlaw the Communist Party (KPD).

### The Reichstag Fire, 27 February 1933

Since 1933 there has been much argument about whether van der Lubbe was indeed responsible for the fire or whether the Nazis started it themselves in order to put the blame on the Communists. Many people in Germany at the time suspected Nazi involvement. A joke went round in Berlin: 'Why did van der Lubbe have no shirt on when he was arrested? Because it was Brown.' 'Brownshirts' was the popular nickname for the SA.

The 1933 election gave the Nazis a 44 percent share of the vote, leaving them 36 seats short of the number they needed for a Reichstag majority. It may appear that the Nazis had failed to get what they wanted. The reality was different. The Nationalists were by now the allies of the Nazis, giving Hitler their 52 Reichstag votes. In addition, the 81 Communists who had been elected were removed from the equation – they were not permitted to take their seats in the Reichstag because the KPD had been banned. The effective outcome of the 1933 election was that 60 percent of Reichstag seats were controlled by the Nazis and their allies.

Artist's impression of the Reichstag Fire, 1933

## The Enabling Act, 23 March 1933

All that remained was for Hitler to amend the 1919 constitution so as to give himself unlimited power. This he proposed to do by getting the Reichstag to pass an Enabling Act which would allow the government to introduce new laws and amend the constitution without the consent of either the Reichstag or the President. As an amendment to the constitution rather than an ordinary law, the Enabling Act had to be passed by a two-thirds majority in the Reichstag. Here Hitler had a difficulty: the Nazis did not have a two-thirds majority in the Reichstag. This meant that he would have to pressurise one of the other major parties into supporting his Enabling Act. The Social Democrats were irreconcilably opposed to it but the Centre Party, after a heated debate, decided to support it. Some in the Centre Party thought that Catholics would earn Hitler's gratitude by giving way over the Enabling Act and would therefore be able to exert influence over him in future. Others believed in Hitler's promises to uphold the position of the Catholic Church in Germany.

The Enabling Act – the Nazis called it the Law to Alleviate the Sufferings of the People and the Country – was passed by the Reichstag by 444–94. Its passage ended any semblance of democracy in Germany.

### Timeline: The last year of the Weimar Republic

| | |
|---|---|
| **13 March, 10 April 1932** | First and second rounds of the Presidential election |
| **30 May 1932** | Brüning's dismissal as Chancellor |
| **1 June 1932** | Von Papen's appointment as Chancellor |
| **20 July 1932** | Unconstitutional seizure of power in the state of Prussia by von Papen |
| **31 July 1932** | Reichstag elections |
| **13 August 1932** | Hitler-Hindenburg meeting: Hitler refused to join von Papen's government |
| **6 November 1932** | Reichstag elections |
| **3 December 1932** | Von Papen removed as Chancellor and replaced by Schleicher |
| **30 January 1933** | Hitler appointed Chancellor |
| **27 February 1933** | Reichstag Fire |
| **5 March 1933** | Reichstag elections |
| **23 March 1933** | Enabling Act passed through Reichstag |

## How did other parties help Hitler into power?

Hitler did not seize power by force but nor did he come into power on the basis of his electoral support alone. He never won a majority in the Reichstag in a free election and even came up short when he resorted to violence and intimidation in March 1933. He was able to become a dictator because others – either deliberately or inadvertently – helped him into power.

### The conservative elites

It was the conservative elites who did more than anyone else to open the way to Nazi rule. They were closer to the Nazis in outlook than any of the other political camps, and after 1930 were only too willing to do business with Hitler. The individuals most responsible for Germany's post-1933 nightmare were Hugenburg, who involved Hitler in the campaign against the Young Plan, Schleicher and von Papen – each of whom tried to use Hitler to further their own ambitions only to find themselves outsmarted. Hindenburg may not have been motivated by personal ambition but was nevertheless responsible for the fateful decision to appoint Hitler Chancellor. These individuals did not, of course, operate in a vacuum: behind them, offering support and encouragement, were the Nationalist Party, the army, the Junkers and big business. Some industrial tycoons gave the Nazis significant financial support. It should in fairness be added that there were individual army generals and more than a few businessmen who were horrified at the thought of Nazi rule.

### The left-wing parties

The two left-wing parties, the Social Democrats and the Communists, were both enemies of Nazism but they were also deeply hostile towards each other. This hostility to some extent blinded them to the seriousness of the Nazi menace. This was especially true of the Communists, who described the Social Democrats as 'social fascists' and claimed they were a bigger danger to the working class than the Nazis. At no point was there any prospect of a united working-class front against the Nazis.

The Social Democrats are open to criticism for another reason: it can be argued that in 1930, by attaching more weight to the interests of their supporters than they did to the preservation of parliamentary government, they helped to create the conditions which made it possible for Hitler to take a back-door route to power.

The Communists can also be criticised for reasons other than their blindness to the seriousness of the Nazi menace. Their lawlessness, their links with Soviet Russia and their unwavering hostility to all other political parties terrified the German middle classes and helped drive the middle classes into the arms of Hitler.

## The Centre Party

Catholics may have been exceptionally reluctant to vote Nazi, but the leaders of the Centre Party were not uncompromising opponents of Hitler. In the early 1930s they indicated that they were prepared to join coalition governments which included the Nazis. In March 1933, the Centre Party smoothed Hitler's path to power by voting for the Enabling Act. By then, however, it was probably too late to stop Hitler.

## The middle-class parties

The middle-class parties, the People's Party and the Democratic Party, were wiped out electorally by the Nazis and rendered powerless. They played no significant part in the intrigues of 1930–1933 that paved the way for Hitler's dictatorship. Both, though, moved sharply to the right in the early 1930s and did nothing to stand up for democratic principles.

# Conclusion: did Hitler come to power legally?

**It can be argued that the requirements of the 1919 constitution were met, at least technically, when Hitler was appointed Chancellor, when the Reichstag Fire decree was issued and when the Enabling Act was passed. It would, however, be nonsensical to suggest that the Nazis always acted within the law in the period up to 1933. From the mid-1920s onwards, they used street violence in a calculated way to destabilise the Republic: scores of people were killed and thousands seriously injured. The wave of Nazi terror which followed Hitler's appointment as Chancellor in 1933 certainly had no basis in law. Hitler's true attitude towards the law was evident when he defended three Nazis convicted of murder as 'nationalist freedom fighters'.**

# Activity: when did Germany cease to be a democracy?

Divide into small groups. Each group should consider one of the following and put forward reasons why it can be seen as the decisive moment in the ending of democratic rule in Germany.

- The end of parliamentary government in 1930
- The introduction of the second version of 'presidential government' in June 1932
- Hitler's appointment as Chancellor in January 1933
- The passage of the Enabling Act in March 1933

Each group should then report back to the whole class.

# Activity: analysing Nazi illegality

You are a journalist working for a Social Democratic Party newspaper published outside Germany after 1933. Write a brief article attacking the Nazis' claim that they came to power entirely by legal means.

---

**Take note**

Using the information in Chapters 3, 4 and 6 as well as the information in this chapter, list the reasons why middle-class Germans lost faith in Weimar democracy. Note down evidence for each reason.

---

**Taking it further**

Disentangling the actions, interactions and motives in 1930–1933 of Hindenburg, Schleicher, Brüning, von Papen and Hitler is no easy matter. For those wishing to study these matters in more depth, there are clear accounts in Chapter 11 of David Williamson, *Germany since 1815* (2005) and Chapter 10 of A.J. Nicholls, *Weimar and the Rise of Hitler* (2000).

# Skills Builder 2: **Planning answers to questions on causation and change**

## Questions on causation

In the AS examination you may be asked questions on causation – questions about what caused historical events to take place.

Some questions may ask you to explain why something happened. For example:

> (A) Why did electoral support for the Nazi Party increase so dramatically in the years 1929–1933?

Other questions on causation will ask you to assess the importance of one cause of an event in relation to other causes. These often begin with 'How far' or 'To what extent'. Here is an example:

> (B) To what extent was the increase in electoral support for the Nazi Party in the years 1929–1933 the result of effective propaganda and electioneering?

## Planning your answer

Before you write your essay you need to make a plan. In the exam you will have to do this very quickly. The first thing to do is to identify the key points you will make in your answer. Let's look at some examples.

When planning an answer to Question (A) you need to note down reasons why electoral support for the Nazis increased in 1929–1933. You can do this in the form of a list or a mind map.

When planning an answer to Question (B) you need to think about the importance of each reason. You could:

- Write a list of all the reasons then number them in order of importance.
- Draw a mind map with 'increased electoral support for the Nazi Party' at the centre and put the most important reasons near the middle and the least important reasons further away.

It is much easier to assess the importance of one factor when you have a list of all relevant factors in front of you.

The information you require for these answers can be found in Chapter 6. Go to Chapter 6 and identify the reasons why electoral support for the Nazi Party increased after 1929.

## Linking the causes

Once you have identified the relevant information and organised it, it is important to highlight links between the reasons.

In making your plan, try grouping together reasons that have links. If you have produced a list of reasons, you may want to rearrange the points where you can identify clear links between them. If you have drawn a mind map, you could draw arrows between the linked points.

## Writing your answer

For Question (A) above, you could write a paragraph on each cause. Alternatively, you might want to start with what you think is the most important cause and then deal with the other causes.

For Question (B) above, it is essential that you refer to the relative importance of different causes, focusing particularly on the role of effective propaganda and electioneering. Remember to answer the question! You might want to deal with the role of propaganda and electioneering first and then assess the importance of other factors which help to account for increased electoral support for the Nazi Party. Make sure you write a separate paragraph for each reason that you identify.

In your concluding paragraph, make sure that you reach a judgment on 'how far' effective propaganda and electioneering were the major reasons for the Nazi electoral breakthrough.

## Questions about change

These questions will require you to explain how far a specified factor changed during a historical period. Examples of this type of question would be:

> (C) How far did the organisation and methods of the Nazi Party change in the years 1920–1929?

> (D) How far did the way in which Germany was governed change in the years 1919–1933?

## Planning your answer

When you plan, organise your ideas in a way that will help you to answer the question.

For instance, for Question (C) you could begin by listing two or three ways in which the organisation and methods of the Nazis changed during the 1920s (for example, the post-1924 'legality' strategy, the imposition of the *Führerprinzip* and the changing role of the SA). Having done that, you could list two or three ways in which organisation and methods stayed the same (for example, Hitler's domination of the NSDAP and the Nazis' willingness to use violence). Alternatively, you could arrange this information on one or two mind maps. Remember that your answer needs to be balanced. Therefore, it should provide points for and against change.

Each of these points will form the basis for one paragraph in your answer. In the last Skills Builder section, you considered the importance of providing specific examples to support your points. Don't forget this!

When you plan, there is no need to organise your material in a chronological way. This may encourage the writing of descriptive or narrative-style answers. Such answers may contain lots of accurate and relevant historical information but may not be directly focused on the question.

## Writing your answer

In Questions (C) and (D) you are asked 'how far' in relation to changes. So in your final paragraph – the conclusion – you will be expected to make a judgment. Based on the historical evidence you have presented in your answer, you should decide, and state, whether you believe the situation mainly changed or stayed the same.

## Activity: How much have you learned?

Here are some examples of questions which deal with causation and change. First, identify the causation questions and give a reason to support your choice. Then identify the questions which deal with change and give a reason for your choice. Finally, choose one 'causation' question and one 'change' question and produce a plan for each, showing how you would organise your answer.

(A) Why did democratic government in Germany survive the problems that it faced in the years 1919–1923?

(B) How far do you agree that Germany became increasingly prosperous in the years 1919–1929?

(C) Why did political extremists of the left and right oppose the Weimar Republic so strongly in the years 1919–1929?

(D) How far did the attitudes of the German middle classes towards the Weimar Republic change in the years 1919–1933?

(E) How far does effective propaganda account for Nazi electoral success in the years 1928–1932?

# Chapter 8 Hitler's 'National Community', 1933–1941

## Key questions

- What did the process of *Gleichschaltung* involve?
- What did the Nazis mean when they spoke of creating a 'National Community' (*Volksgemeinschaft*)?
- What methods were used to create a 'National Community'?
- Who was excluded from the 'National Community', and how were they treated?
- How successful was the Nazi attempt to create a 'National Community'?

Nazism was heavily influenced by Social Darwinism, a 19th century doctrine which held that nations were the same as biological species, competing against each other in a struggle for existence in which only the fittest would survive. The implication was that weak and unfit nations would be conquered. The Nazis believed that under democratic rule Germany could never triumph in this struggle for existence. Democratic Germany, they argued, was weak because it was divided – and it was divided mainly because people had been indoctrinated into thinking of themselves primarily as workers or Catholics rather than as Germans. The solution, said the Nazis, was to create a unified *Volksgemeinschaft* ('National Community') in which people would think of themselves first and foremost as Germans and would regard service to the nation as their most important duty. Turning the *Volksgemeinschaft* idea into a reality was one of the Nazis' main aims when they got into power. Much of what they did in the field of domestic policy in the 1930s was directed towards the achievement of this aim. The goal of creating a *Volksgemeinschaft* lay behind three of the Nazis' most significant undertakings after 1933: the subjection of German institutions in 1933–1934 to the process of so-called ***Gleichschaltung***; the sustained drive to heighten national awareness spearheaded by Goebbels' Ministry of Propaganda and National Enlightenment; and the persecution of a range of minorities – Jews, Roma and Sinti, homosexuals and the disabled – on the basis that they were not fit to belong to the 'National Community'.

## Glossary

### *Gleichschaltung*

Literally, this means 'the process of switching on to the same wavelength' or 'bringing into line'. It is often translated into English as 'coordination'. In relation to Nazi Germany, it is used to describe the process which took place in 1933–1934 when the country's major institutions and organisations were either abolished or Nazified.

## *Gleichschaltung*, 1933–1934

### *Gleichschaltung* and political parties

Before 1933 Hitler had attacked the 'sectional' political parties of the Weimar Republic as one of the main causes of Germany's disunity and weakness. After he achieved supreme power they became one of his first targets. In June 1933 the Social Democratic Party was outlawed – a fate that had already befallen the Communists. The other Weimar parties – the Nationalists, the People's Party, the Democratic Party and the Centre Party – were not formally outlawed but were pressured into dissolving themselves. The Nazis then introduced a Law Against the Formation of New Parties (July 1933). This made Germany officially a one-party state. Hitler, boasted Propaganda Minister Goebbels in a speech in mid-1933, had destroyed the Weimar's multi-party system and unified the German people into one will.

The Social Democratic Party lasted a few weeks longer than its associated trade union movement. The Nazis disbanded the trade unions in May 1933. In the 1920s Germany's socialist trade unions had been a powerful force in the land: now they disappeared overnight.

## Violence and terror

The suppression of Germany's political left was not merely an administrative exercise. It involved a great deal of violence and terror. In mid-1933 hundreds of socialists and Communists were murdered by the SA, often after being abducted and taken to so-called 'wild camps' set up in disused buildings. When the goings-on in these makeshift camps became the subject of adverse publicity, Hitler shut them down and handed responsibility for neutralising potential threats to his regime to **Heinrich Himmler's SS**. This led to the construction in 1933 of a network of over 80 concentration camps. The camp at Dachau, near Munich, was the model on which all the others were based. Although people died in the concentration camps, the camps were not built for the purpose of extermination. Their purpose, to begin with at least, was to keep known opponents of the Nazi regime in what was called 'protective custody'. Most camp inmates in 1933 were Communists and Social Democrats.

> ### Heinrich Himmler and the SS
>
> A cold-blooded, ambitious and ruthless figure, Heinrich Himmler (1900–1945) was appointed leader of the SS in 1929. At the time the role of the SS was limited. It was Hitler's personal bodyguard, a role reflected in its name: SS stands for *Schutzstaffel* or 'protection squad'. Under Himmler's leadership, however, its importance grew enormously. By 1939 Himmler and the SS not only controlled the concentration camp network but also all of Germany's police forces – including the *Gestapo*, Nazi Germany's secret police. In 1941 the SS was given responsibility for carrying out what the Nazis called the 'final solution' of 'the Jewish question' – the extermination of the Jews of Europe.

## *Gleichschaltung* and the churches

The Nazis did not regard Christian belief as fully compatible with membership of the *Volksgemeinschaft*. They feared that in the event of conflict between church and state, Christians could not be relied upon to put the state first. But they saw no need to rush into conflict with the churches: they saw them as a less divisive influence than political parties and they knew that any resort to the kind of strong-arm tactics used elsewhere would cause an outcry. So there was no full-blooded attack on the churches in 1933–1934 – but nor were they left to their own devices. The Protestant churches – a soft target from the Nazi point of view because many of their middle-class members had voted for Hitler in the elections of the early 1930s – were persuaded in 1933 to organise themselves into a Reich Church with a Reich Bishop, Ludwig Müller, at its head. A minority of German Protestants, however, refused to accept Müller's leadership and set up an organisation of their own, the Confessional Church. So far as the Catholic Church was concerned, Hitler by-passed the German bishops and dealt directly with the Pope. In 1933 an agreement was reached between the Nazis and the Vatican: the Nazis promised to allow the Catholic Church to carry on its religious work without interference, and the Pope ordered German priests to stay out of politics.

### Take note

As you read through this section on *Gleichschaltung*, construct a three-column table identifying (i) the organisations or institutions which were abolished as part of the *Gleichschaltung* process, (ii) those which were remodelled and (iii) those which were largely left alone. How would you account for these differences of treatment?

Heinrich Himmler in 1938

## The SA and the SS

The SA and the SS are not to be confused. The brown-uniformed SA was a mass-membership Nazi paramilitary organisation which peaked in terms of size and influence in the early 1930s, under the leadership of Ernst Röhm. The black-uniformed SS was an elite formation which began its existence in the 1920s as Hitler's personal bodyguard, but grew in size and importance after 1933. Headed by the ambitious Heinrich Himmler, it gained responsibility for policing and the concentration camps, among other things.

## Biography

### Ernst Röhm
(1887–1934)

Ernst Röhm joined the Nazi party right at the start in 1920. He had previously been an army officer and, in 1919, a fighter in one of the Free Corps. He took part in the Munich *putsch* in 1923 and then went off to fight as a mercenary in South America. Hitler made him head of the SA in 1931. Under his leadership the SA quickly grew in size. Röhm was a dynamic figure but he was also wild and undisciplined.

After 1933 Hitler faced significant opposition from within the Christian churches. Martin Niemöller, the former First World War submarine captain and one-time Nazi sympathiser who headed the Confessional Church, became an open critic of Nazi anti-Semitism. In 1937 he was arrested and sent to a concentration camp. Some of Niemöller's associates in the Confessional Church, notably Dietrich Bonhoeffer and Karl Barth, were equally courageous. Individual Catholic priests also spoke out against Nazism. By 1937 hundreds of Catholic priests had been arrested and imprisoned. These arrests, together with Nazi breaches of the promise made in 1933 not to interfere with Catholic institutions, such as youth organisations, led Pope Pius XI to condemn Hitler in a famous statement called '*Mit brennender Sorge*' ('With burning anxiety'). It does, however, need to be borne in mind that there was no all-out conflict between the Nazi regime and the Christian churches. Relations deteriorated, but churches remained open and services were held.

The process of *Gleichschaltung* was not confined to political parties, the trade unions and the churches. Local government, the civil service, the justice system, the police, education and the media were among the other institutions affected. In the majority of cases organisations were remodelled by the Nazis rather than abolished: abolition was reserved for those seen as an affront to the 'National Community'. Apart from the Catholic Church, the only institution to escape full-blown Nazification in 1933–1934 was the army, which Hitler saw as too powerful to offend. Its turn was to come in 1938.

## The 'Night of the Long Knives', 1934

In 1933–1934 Hitler had to contend with a divisive influence in his own ranks: the SA. The SA leadership, headed by **Ernst Röhm**, began to make demands Hitler was unwilling to meet.

- The SA, nearly three million strong in 1933, wanted to merge with the much smaller German army. Since the SA were street brawlers and not trained soldiers, Hitler feared that a merger would undermine the discipline and effectiveness of Germany's armed forces.

- The SA leaders were socialistic or 'left-wing' Nazis who took the anti-capitalist elements of the party's programme seriously. In 1933 they began to call for a 'second revolution' – the first revolution being the Nazi seizure of power and the destruction of the KPD and SPD. The target of this 'second revolution' was to be big business. Hitler, however, was looking to involve Germany's industrial leaders in his plans to rebuild the country's military strength. He had no intention of waging war on big business.

These demands put the SA leadership on collision course with Hitler. Amid mounting tension, Hitler struck. On 30 June 1934 he ordered the murder of over fifty of the SA's top leaders, Röhm included. At the same time, he settled some old scores: Gustav von Kahr, Gregor Strasser and Kurt von Schleicher were also murdered. All of the killings were carried out by the SS.

This bloodbath, soon dubbed the Night of the Long Knives, was seen outside Germany as a shocking act of political gangsterism. Inside Germany, it did Hitler's reputation no harm at all: the SA leaders were deeply unpopular with the wider public because they were felt to be greedy and corrupt. The feeling seems to have been that Hitler had rid the Nazi party of its worst elements. The SA continued to exist after the Night of Long Knives, but it had neither power nor influence or a clear role.

The Night of the Long Knives in some ways marked the end of Hitler's seizure of power. His thoughts now turned to foreign affairs and war.

### Timeline: *Gleichschaltung* 1933–1934

| | |
|---|---|
| **Mar 1933** | Communist Party outlawed |
| **May 1933** | Abolition of trade unions |
| **Jun 1933** | Social Democratic Party outlawed |
| **Jul 1933** | Law Against the Formation of New Parties |
| **Jul 1933** | Agreement ('*concordat*') between Nazi Germany and the Vatican |
| **Jul 1933** | Establishment of the Protestant 'Reich Church' |
| **30 Jun–2 Jul 1934** | 'Night of the Long Knives' |

## Propaganda and popular culture

### How did propaganda contribute to the attempt to create a *Volksgemeinschaft*?

Goebbels was made Minister of Propaganda and National Enlightenment soon after the March 1933 election. On appointment he declared that his primary goal was to foster a sense of unity among the German people. His ministry, he said, had 'no other aim than to unite the nation behind the ideal of the national revolution'. This it tried to do using a variety of techniques.

- There was much use of posters and slogans to promote a sense of unity. Examples of slogans include 'The community before the individual' and 'One Nation! One People! One Leader!'

- A personality cult was built up around Hitler. Germans were urged to hero-worship him as the master-builder of the 'National Community'. Nazi propaganda also claimed that by sacrificing family life for the sake of his country Hitler exemplified the ideal of putting community before self. The historian Ian Kershaw calls the propaganda image of Hitler which Goebbels constructed 'the Hitler myth'.

- Political rituals or celebrations in the form of rallies, marches and parades were used to create the impression that Germany was united behind Hitler. In Nazi Germany elaborately staged celebrations or rituals were regular events.

**Take note**

Using the information contained in Chapters 5 and 7, explain why Hitler bore grudges against Gustav von Kahr, Gregor Strasser and Kurt von Schleicher.

**Take note**

Write three sentences, giving **one** example in each of the methods used by the Nazis to try to break down the barriers to *Volksgemeinschaft* created by (i) social class, (ii) religion and (iii) region.

| | |
|---|---|
| **30 January** | Day of the Seizure of Power |
| **24 February** | Founding of the Nazi Party Day |
| **16 March** | Heroes' Remembrance Day (remembrance of those killed in the 1914–1918 war) |
| **20 April** | Hitler's Birthday |
| **1 May** | National Labour Day |
| **May** | Mothering Sunday |
| **September** | Annual Nazi Party Rally at Nuremberg |
| **9 November** | Anniversary of the Munich *putsch* |

Main celebrations in the Nazi political calendar

- The Nazis introduced a Winter Aid Programme in which better-off Germans were encouraged to give money, food and clothing to poverty-stricken 'national comrades'. The idea was to persuade Germans that they were part of a cohesive society in which people looked out for each other.

- Goebbels believed that the written word was not as effective an instrument of propaganda as the spoken word or film. The Nazis therefore made extensive use of radio and cinema in their efforts to inspire feelings of solidarity among the German people. They ensured that practically every household had access to a radio by marketing a low-cost 'People's Receiver'. Nazi radio broadcasts could also be heard in factories and other public places through loudspeakers which were put up for the purpose.

Josef Goebbels in 1934

Needless to say, the Nazis did not allow any material to be put into the public domain which conflicted with their insistence that divisions of class, religion and region were being broken down. Here the key organisation was the Reich Chamber of Culture, part of Goebbels' Ministry of Propaganda. Anyone wanting to work in film, journalism, radio or the arts had to be a member of the Chamber of Culture. Only those who were in sympathy with the Nazis were allowed to join. Non-members could not get their work published or performed.

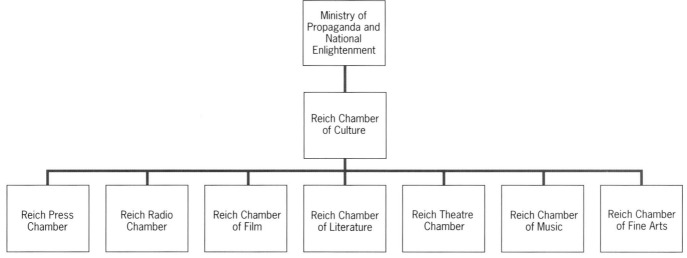

The Reich Chamber of Culture

## Popular culture

Propaganda was not the only device used by the Nazis to try to integrate Germans into a 'National Community'. They also made a determined effort to sell the *Volksgemeinschaft* idea to the working classes through the KdF (*Kraft durch Freude:* 'Strength through Joy') movement. The KdF was part of the German Labour Front, the organisation the Nazis established in 1933 to replace the trade unions. In part the role of the KdF was to fill a gap left in the lives of working-class families by the liquidation of the Social Democratic and Communist parties. Before 1933 these parties had offered their supporters a wide range of leisure and cultural opportunities in the form of sports leagues, choirs, evening classes and the like: after 1933 this sort of provision was made by the KdF.

The KdF did not, however, restrict itself to replacing Social Democratic or Communist arrangements with Nazi ones. It came up with initiatives of its own which were more ambitious than anything which had existed before 1933. It became heavily involved in the tourism business, sponsoring cheap travel inside Germany and providing opportunities for travel abroad on KdF cruise ships. Behind these seemingly harmless schemes there were political motives: the Nazis hoped that travel inside Germany would help to break down people's regional loyalties, and that foreign travel would convince the working classes that in the *Volksgemeinschaft* they would have opportunities which were previously available only to the rich. Another attention-grabbing KdF initiative, launched in 1938, was the *Volkswagen* or 'People's Car' scheme. The launch slogan was 'a Volkswagen for every German'. Would-be buyers were invited to order their Volkswagen before it went into production and to start paying for it at the rate of five marks per week. Dazzled by the almost unimaginable luxury of private car ownership, over 300,000 people signed up. None of them ever received a car or got their money back: the whole project was scrapped when war broke out because the Volkswagen plant was needed to produce military vehicles.

'You must save 5 marks a week if you want to drive your own car'

## Persecution and genocide: Nazi anti-Semitism, 1933–1945

### Timeline: Persecution of Jews in Germany, 1933–1939

| 1 April 1933 | One-day boycott of Jewish shops |
|---|---|
| 7 April 1933 | Law for the Restoration of the Professional Civil Service |
| 10 May 1933 | Public burning in Berlin of books by Jewish, socialist and other authors |
| 15 Sept 1935 | Nuremberg Laws |
| April 1938 | Beginnings of Goering's 'Aryanisation' policy |
| 9 Nov 1938 | *Kristallnacht*; billion-mark fine imposed on the Jewish community |

### Why were Germany's Jews excluded from the 'National Community'?

Membership of the Nazi 'National Community' was not open to everyone. There were requirements which had to be met. The most basic requirement arose out of the Nazis' racial theories. Only **Aryans** could belong to the *Volksgemeinschaft*. This meant the exclusion of those categorised as non-Aryans: Jews, and Germany's gypsies – the Roma and Sinti. But this was not all. Jews, said the Nazis, were enemies of the Aryan *Volksgemeinschaft*, seeking actively to destroy it.

- The Jews, according to the Nazis, were a race, not a religious group, and were bent on world domination.

- Jews, claimed the Nazis, would resort to any means to further their objectives. These included using Communism as a front to hide behind. Hitler was convinced that Russian Communism was controlled by Jews. He believed in the existence of a 'Jewish-Bolshevik conspiracy' to take over the world. Another Nazi allegation was that Jews had conspired to win control of Germany's financial institutions.

### Glossary

**Aryans**

According to Nazi race theory, there were three main racial groups in Europe: the Aryans (or the 'Nordic' or 'Germanic' race, in its purest form distinguished physically by blond hair and blue eyes), the Latin race (French, Spanish, Italians) and the 'sub-human' Slavs. The Nazis also viewed Europe's ten million Jews as a distinct race.

- The Nazis believed that Germany's Jews, acting in the interests of **world Jewry**, had done all that they could to bring about the country's defeat in the 1914–1918 war.

These claims were used by the Nazis to justify persecution, terrorisation and, ultimately, **genocide**.

### Germany's Jewish community

There was no substance to the Nazis' claims about the power and influence of Germany's Jewish community. They were pure fantasy.

- In 1933 only 0.7 percent of Germany's population was Jewish. Germany's Jews were not only a small minority but a diminishing one as well: numbers were falling as a result of low birth rates and the increasing frequency of marriages between Jews and non-Jews.

- Jews did not dominate German business life as the Nazis alleged. They were, if anything, under-represented in the upper reaches of industry and finance. The occupations in which Germany's Jews were most likely to be found were the middle-class professions – medicine, law, teaching and journalism – and some branches of commerce, particularly retailing.

- Germany's Jews were an assimilated community. Its members saw no incompatibility between their faith and their nationality. Significantly, the leading Jewish organisation in Germany in the early 20th century was called the Union of German Citizens of Jewish Faith. In the 1914–1918 war 100,000 of Germany's half-million strong Jewish community served in the German army: 12,000 of them died in action.

### The persecution of Germany's Jews, 1933–1939

The earliest Nazi moves against Germany's Jews were vicious but uncoordinated. In spring 1933 local SA units, acting largely on their own initiative, went on the rampage, beating up Jews and destroying Jewish property. This left the impression that the Nazi leadership was unable to control its rank-and-file supporters. In order to regain the initiative, Hitler ordered a one-day boycott of Jewish shops on 1 April 1933. A few days later on 7 April 1933 the Nazi government issued its first anti-Jewish decree, the hastily drafted Law for the Restoration of the Professional Civil Service. Among other things, this ordered the dismissal of all non-Aryan civil servants. There was a partial government climbdown after Hindenburg, still Germany's President, intervened on behalf of Jewish war veterans: Jews who had fought in the trenches were allowed to keep their jobs.

1934 saw a pause in Nazi persecution of the Jews but in 1935 Hitler returned to the attack. He was prompted to do so by demands for a more aggressive anti-Jewish policy from the SA, still smarting from the murder of its leaders on the 'Night of the Long Knives'. Hitler's response was to announce two new anti-Jewish laws at the annual Nazi party rally at Nuremberg.

- The Reich Citizenship Law deprived Jews of German citizenship and turned them into aliens in their own country.

- The Law for the Protection of German Blood and Honour outlawed marriage between Jews and non-Jews and made sexual relations between Jews and non-Jews outside marriage a criminal offence.

These Nuremberg Laws were put together in a mere two days and were imprecise. They contained no definition of who counted as a Jew. Later in 1935 the Nazis introduced a further law, the Supplementary Decree to the Reich Citizenship Law, to clarify this point. A Jew was defined as someone with three or four Jewish grandparents. People with one or two Jewish grandparents were labelled *Mischlinge* ('hybrids'). *Mischlinge* with one Jewish grandparent largely escaped persecution but those with two did not.

In 1931 Berlin was chosen to host the 1936 Olympic Games. Hitler saw the Olympics as an opportunity to showcase the Nazi regime and its alleged achievements. He did not want them to be marred by controversy. As a result, anti-Semitic activity was scaled down. All signs of anti-Semitism in public places in Germany – notices, posters and the like – were removed.

In 1937–1938 it became clear that a new onslaught on Germany's Jews was in the offing. Himmler, the ambitious head of the SS, began to interest himself in Jewish policy, arguing that Germany should be made 'Jew-free' by terrorising Jews into leaving the country. By contrast, Herman Goering, appointed Germany's economic supremo in 1936 (see page 82), favoured a policy of 'Aryanisation' – stripping Jews of their property, selling it to non-Jews and investing the proceeds in economic development. Then Goebbels intervened. On 9 November 1938, using as a pretext the murder of a German diplomat in Paris by a Jewish teenager, Goebbels, with Hitler's approval, launched the **pogrom** which became known as ***Kristallnacht***. It was an outburst of violence and destruction: at least 90 Jews were killed; hundreds more were beaten up; over 200 synagogues were destroyed by fire and nearly 8,000 Jewish businesses were smashed and looted. The Nazi leadership tried to pretend that *Kristallnacht* was an unprompted popular response to the Paris murder, but few were fooled.

The 1938 pogrom was followed by a rash of new anti-Semitic laws, notably the Decree Excluding Jews from German Economic Life, which prevented Jews from running businesses, and decrees excluding Jews from many public places. In addition, a collective fine of one billion marks was levied on the Jewish community as a punishment for the Paris murder and 30,000 Jewish men were rounded up and sent to concentration camps.

## How coherent were Nazi anti-Jewish policies before 1939?

Clearly the position of Germany's Jews deteriorated in the 1930s. It did not, however, deteriorate steadily or progressively. The Nazis' anti-Jewish policies before 1939 were unsystematic, chaotic even.

### Glossary

**Pogrom**

This is a word used to describe organised, often government-encouraged, mob attacks on minority populations, particularly Jews. It comes from a Russian word meaning 'to destroy'.

**Kristallnacht**

*Kristallnacht* means 'crystal night', but is also known as 'the night of broken glass'. The events of 9 November 1938 were given this name on account of the broken glass which covered the shopping streets of Germany's major cities after Nazis had smashed the shop-fronts of thousands of Jewish-owned stores.

## Hitler and the Jews

There is much debate among historians about whether Hitler intended genocide from the beginning or whether he only decided finally on a policy of genocide after the outbreak of war in 1939. There was certainly no active planning for genocide in the 1930s: Hitler seemed to favour a policy of making Germany 'Jew-free' by forced emigration. As late as 1940 the Nazis devised a plan to solve 'the Jewish problem' by forcing European Jews to migrate to the French colony of Madagascar.

## Glossary

### *Einsatzgruppen*

Part of Himmler's SS. Each *Einsatzgruppe* consisted of between 600 and 1000 men and was divided up into three or four sub-units called *Einsatzkommando*. Members of the *Einsatzgruppen* were drawn from different branches of the SS. Most were soldiers from the military force known as the *Waffen SS*, but others came from the various SS-controlled police forces – the *Gestapo*, the SD or *Sicherheitsdienst* ('security service') and the Order Police. The officers who led the *Einsatzgruppen* were for the most part highly educated: two-thirds of them had been to university.

- There was no settled policy. Initiative followed initiative in bewildering fashion. At one time or another these initiatives included the boycotting of Jewish retailers, discriminatory laws, forced emigration, dispossession and, in 1938, physical attack. In the later 1930s there was also competition between rival approaches, with Himmler and Goering battling for control of Jewish policy.

- The initiatives sometimes cut across each other. Goering, for example, was furious with Goebbels after *Kristallnacht* because he could not strip Jews of their property if it had been destroyed.

- The intensity of persecution varied. Germany's Jews came under savage attack in 1933, 1935 and 1938–1939 but there were quiet years, relatively speaking, in 1934 and 1936–1937.

### Towards genocide

In 1939–1941 the context of Nazi Jewish policy changed in two important ways.

1. Germany was now at war. As a result of the invasions of Poland (1939) and Russia (1941), the Nazis had at their mercy over five million Jews who had not previously been at risk.

2. In occupied Poland and Russia the Nazis could operate out of public view. In Germany in the 1930s their actions were observable by foreign diplomats and journalists and known to everyone.

In these circumstances, Nazi policy moved first towards mass murder and then towards systematic genocide.

- In September 1939 SS *Einsatzgruppen* ('task forces') followed the German armies into Poland. Their task was to eliminate potential resisters. By the end of 1939 they had butchered over 50,000 Polish civilians – many, but not all, of them Jews.

- From late 1939 onwards, Poland's Jews were herded into **ghettoes** as an interim measure while the Nazi leadership pondered their ultimate fate. A million Jews died in these ghettoes as a result of malnutrition and disease.

- In summer 1941 the *Einsatzgruppen* followed the German armies into Soviet Russia. Jews were specifically targeted. There were wholesale killings, mostly by shooting: over a million Jews died.

- Hitler did not sign written orders for either 'ghettoisation' or mass shootings, but without any doubt authorised both.

- In mid-1941, against the background of mass murder in Poland and Russia, the Nazi leadership turned its attention to the fate of Jews in other parts of Nazi-occupied Europe. It was decided that they should be rounded up and taken to extermination camps to be sited in Poland. Soon afterwards (January 1942) Heydrich, Himmler's deputy, summoned 15 top Nazi officials to a conference at Wannsee, on the outskirts of Berlin, to brief them on their part in this 'new solution'.

The construction of extermination camps at Treblinka, Sobibor and Chelmno followed. Existing concentration camps, such as Auschwitz, and camps already under construction, such as Belzec and Majdanek, were fitted with gas chambers for the purpose of mass murder.

> ### Recollections of Rudolf Hoess, the first commandant of Auschwitz
>
> 'In the summer of 1941 – I can't remember the exact date – I was suddenly summoned to see Himmler. He received me and said "Hitler has ordered that the Jewish question be solved once and for all and that we, the SS, are to implement that order. Our existing facilities in the East are not in a position to carry out the large actions that are anticipated. I have therefore earmarked Auschwitz for this purpose, both because of its good position as regards communication and because the area can easily be isolated and camouflaged. You will treat this order as absolutely secret." '

## Other persecutions

### Roma and Sinti

Germany's 35,000 Roma and Sinti ('gypsies') were excluded from the *Volksgemeinschaft* on the same basis as Jews: they were deemed to be non-Aryans. They were also stereotyped as work shy and criminal. Their treatment at the hands of the Nazis paralleled that of the Jews. After 1933 the Roma and Sinti were persecuted, with many being sent to concentration camps. The 1935 Nuremberg Laws were applied to them as they were to Jews. Persecution intensified following the establishment in 1936 of the Reich Central Office to Combat the Gypsy Nuisance. After 1939 persecution gave way to genocide. German Roma and Sinti, together with others from across Nazi-occupied Europe, were deported to extermination camps in Poland. Estimates of the number killed in the camps vary between 220,000 and 500,000.

### Disabled people

The mentally ill and physically disabled were not excluded from the *Volksgemeinschaft* because they were non-Aryans. The Nazis maintained they were unfit to belong to the 'National Community' on different grounds: they were 'genetically defective' and as such were a source of weakness. This view was based on the theories of the **eugenics movement**. In addition, the Nazis saw the mentally ill and physically disabled as a burden on society – 'useless mouths', in Hitler's phrase.

Hitler made it clear in *Mein Kampf* that he believed in the sterilisation of the 'genetically defective'. In power he quickly put his beliefs into practice. The Law for the Prevention of Hereditarily Diseased Offspring (July 1933) provided for the compulsory sterilisation of the seriously mentally ill, epileptics, people born blind or deaf, those born with severe physical deformities and alcoholics. It led to the sterilisation of some 400,000 people.

### Glossary

#### Ghetto

A ghetto is part of a city inhabited by people of the same ethnic group, religion or social class. Ghettoes can result from poverty and disadvantage, but the Nazi ghettoes were created by design.

### Glossary

#### The eugenics movement

This movement was influential in the late 19th and early 20th centuries – not only in Germany but in the USA and Britain as well. Its supporters believed that the quality of a human population could be improved through selective breeding. They argued that the 'fit' should be encouraged to have children and the 'unfit' prevented from having children.

**Take note**

Using your own words, explain briefly the meaning of each of the following: *Volksgemeinschaft*; *Gleichschaltung*; *Mischlinge*; *Kraft durch Freude*; *Kristallnacht*; *Einsatzgruppen*.

The Nazis made no secret of their mass sterilisation programme. It was a different matter when they launched Operation T-4 in 1939. This was a plan for mass murder – the planners preferred the term 'euthanasia' – which targeted seriously ill mental hospital in-patients. Here the Nazis operated out of public view. Between 1939 and 1941 70,000 people were killed, mostly by gassing. The T-4 programme was halted when news of it leaked out and the Nazi leadership was publicly criticised, notably by Clemens von Galen, the Catholic Bishop of Münster. Unofficially, however, 'euthanasia' programmes of one kind or another continued.

### Homosexuals

Before 1933 homosexuality had been no bar to advancement within the Nazi party. The SA boss Ernst Röhm and several of his lieutenants were more or less openly gay. When the Nazis were in power it was different. Homosexuals were excluded from the 'National Community' on the grounds that they were 'deviants' who were failing in their duty to the Third Reich by not producing children. Some 50,000 German men were arrested for homosexual offences in the 1930s: around 15,000 of them ended up in concentration camps.

## Conclusion: how successful were the Nazis in creating a *Volksgemeinschaft* in the 1930s?

The *Volksgemeinschaft* project was a hugely ambitious undertaking. Breaking down the barriers of class, religion and region required changes of a fundamental kind in the mind-set of millions of German people. Turning middle-aged and elderly people who had supported the Communists or Social Democrats throughout their lives into enthusiastic Nazis was a near-impossible task. In some ways, though, the project had its successes.

- The idea of a *Volksgemeinschaft* undoubtedly appealed to middle-class Germans wearied by the squabbles and divisions of the 1920s.

- There is a lot of evidence which suggests that working-class Germans appreciated the leisure opportunities made available by the 'Strength through Joy' organisation. No doubt they were appreciative too of the increased holiday entitlements they received in the Nazi era and of Nazi attempts to improve factory conditions. The very poorest also benefited from 'Winter Aid', a Nazi-organised charitable enterprise.

- Hitler enjoyed high levels of personal popularity throughout the 1930s. Goebbels' depiction of the *Führer* in Nazi propaganda as the selfless leader of a unified nation paid dividends.

- There was little active resistance to Nazi rule in the 1930s. Active resistance in these years added up to little more than attempts by the Communists and Social Democrats to keep going as underground organisations, protests by some church leaders on specific issues and the emergence of a handful of dissident youth groups.

*Führer*

In 1933–1934 Hindenburg kept the title of President and remained Germany's official head of state. Hitler's official title during these years was Chancellor. When Hindenburg died in 1934, Hitler abolished the Presidency and gave himself the new title of 'Führer (leader) and Reich Chancellor'. Between 1934 and 1945 Hitler was both Germany's head of state and its head of government.

Active resistance was limited mainly because of fear of the Nazi secret police forces. But the lack of active resistance certainly does not mean that all Germans were enthusiastic supporters of Nazi rule. Some showed their distaste for Nazism by engaging in acts of minor dissent, such as refusing to give the *Heil Hitler!* salute. Others who disliked Nazism shut themselves off from politics and public life and withdrew entirely into private and family life. This was known as 'inner emigration'.

Ultimately, however, the attempt to construct a *Volksgemeinschaft* was a failure:

- German society did not become more equal in any real sense in the 1930s. Differences of wealth and power remained. The Nazis did not pretend otherwise. They said the *Volksgemeinschaft* was not about people being equal but about them being equally valued. This left them vulnerable to the charge that the changes they made were purely cosmetic.

- The Nazis failed to integrate the working classes into the 'National Community'. Workers and their families may have enjoyed their KdF-sponsored days out but this did not mean that they were wholly won over to Nazism. Class-based attitudes certainly did not disappear. 'Under the propaganda varnish of the National Community', says historian Ian Kershaw, 'old antagonisms continued unabated.' (2001)

- Historical research suggests that religious affiliations and regional identities remained strong in 1930s Germany.

- Nazi attempts to foster a sense of unity by scapegoating and persecuting Jews and other minorities appear to have been largely unsuccessful. Germans may not have sprung to the defence of persecuted minorities – fear of the SS terror apparatus helped see to that – but this does not mean that all of them viewed what went on with enthusiasm.

## Activity: The Nazi *Volksgemeinschaft*

- How effective was Nazi propaganda in the years 1933–1939?

- How and why did Nazi anti-Jewish policy change direction in 1939–1941?

- Draw up a table indicating (i) the ways in which the Nazi *Volksgemeinschaft* project can be said to have achieved its objectives and (ii) the ways in which it failed. Use your table as the basis for writing a short paragraph which assesses the extent to which the *Volksgemeinchaft* project was a failure.

---

### Taking it further

On the website of the United States Holocaust Memorial Museum there are a number of highly accessible online exhibitions which explore some of the themes treated in this chapter in more depth. Particularly relevant are *Deadly Medicine: Creating the Master Race*; *States of Deception: The Power of Nazi Propaganda*; and *Kristallnacht: The November 1938 Pogroms*. Use these exhibitions to research the following questions:

- How did ordinary Germans react to the persecution of minorities?
- How and why did the Nazis persecute other minorities, such as 'asocials' and Jehovah's Witnesses?

# Chapter 9 Building the future: women, education and young people in Nazi Germany

## Key questions

- Why did the Nazis attach so much importance to women and the young?
- How much impact did Nazi policies towards women have?
- How did the Nazis change Germany's educational system?
- How much impact did Nazi youth policies have?

Hitler made it clear in *Mein Kampf* that once he got into power he would wage aggressive war. He knew that his aim of securing 'land and soil' for Germany at the expense of Soviet Russia could never be realised by peaceful means. He also expected that Germany would have to fight in order to hold on to its conquests. Germany's future, he predicted, would be one of 'eternal struggle'. The belief that Germany would have to fight endlessly for its existence had a powerful influence on the Nazis' attitudes to women and to the young. These attitudes were uncomplicated. The duty of women, said the Nazis, was to meet the manpower needs of the German army by having children in large numbers. As for young men, their duty was to fight in wars. Nazi efforts to equip the younger generation to carry out its duties involved a lot of emphasis on developing toughness, resilience and physical fitness. There was also an emphasis on getting the younger generation to believe totally in Nazi ideas. Hitler spoke of creating a Nazi empire which would last for a thousand years. This meant raising generation after generation of fanatical Nazis.

### Take note

Construct a table with three rows labelled 'Policy towards women', 'Education policy' and 'Youth policy' and three columns headed 'Aims', 'Methods' and 'Success'. As you read this chapter, add information to each cell in the table.

### Timeline

| 1933 | Dismissal of Jewish and 'unreliable' teachers from schools<br>Introduction of the Marriage Loan Scheme<br>Baldur von Schirach named 'Youth Leader of the German Reich' |
|------|---|
| 1936 | Law on the Hitler Youth introduced<br>Catholic Youth Association outlawed |
| 1938 | Introduction of the Mother Cross award |

## Women in Nazi Germany

### The Weimar era

The 1920s were years of progress for German women.

- In politics, the Weimar constitution gave women the right to vote for the first time. It also enabled women to become members of the Reichstag. The percentage of female members of the Reichstag in the 1920s was much higher than the number of female MPs in Britain in the same period.

- There were also gains in the economic field. The number of women in paid employment rose sharply in the early 1920s, filling the gaps left by the four million men who had been killed or disabled in the 1914–1918 war.

- There was more social freedom, too, in matters such as dress and going out. The Weimar 'new woman' with her short hair, short skirt and cigarette became the object of much comment in newspapers and magazines.

The stylish 'new woman' was viewed with alarm by right-wing Germans. There were complaints that German women were running wild. In reality, the 'new woman' was a rarity outside of the big cities.

## What ideas did the Nazis have about the role of women?

The Nazis did not hide their contempt for the 'new woman' of the 1920s. In their view, the 'new woman' was selfish and immoral. The Nazis argued that the key role of women was not to make a contribution in the world of paid work but to serve their country by devoting themselves to child-bearing and child-rearing. This domestic role, they said, was what nature intended for women. They denied that it involved relegating women to a status inferior to that of men. The Nazis acknowledged that the roles of men and women were different but claimed that these roles complemented each other and were equally important. The reality, of course, was that under Nazism German women lived in a strongly male-dominated society and were denied opportunities. In addition, women beyond their child-bearing years were regarded as expendable. In the war years, for example, older women were often given the most dangerous jobs in munitions factories on the basis that they were of less value to the state than others.

> ### Hitler on the role of women, 1934
>
> 'If one says that man's world is his struggle, his readiness to act on behalf of the community, then one could say that the world of the woman is a smaller one. For her world is her husband, her family, her children, and her home. But where would the larger world be if no one wanted to look after the little world? This large world cannot exist, if the little world is not stable. We feel it is not appropriate when woman forces her way into the man's world; instead we perceive it as natural when these two worlds remain separate.'

## 'Pronatalism'

'Pronatalism' is the policy or practice of encouraging child-bearing and glorifying parenthood. The Nazis were very strongly committed to 'pronatalism'. They regarded Germany's population as it was in 1933 as much too small for their purposes. Germany, they reasoned, could not hope to succeed in its struggle for existence unless it had much bigger reserves of manpower.

> **Take note**
>
> 1. Read the section on the Nazis' ideas about women and summarise these attitudes in your own words.
> 2. As you read the following sections, make a list of all the policies introduced by the Nazis that were consistent with their attitudes to women, and another list of those that were inconsistent with their attitudes and beliefs.
> 3. Write a sentence to answer the question: How consistent were Nazi policies towards women?

### Gertrud Schlotz-Klink
#### (1902–1999)

Gertrud Schlotz-Klink was the highest-ranking female political figure in Hitler's Germany. In 1934 she was given the title of leader of all National Socialist women. This high-sounding title concealed the fact that she had little real power. Schlotz-Klink married three times and had eleven children.

Gertrude Schlotz-Klink addresses a Nazi rally in 1937

### Germany's birth rate

A country's annual birth rate is calculated by working out how many children are born per thousand of the population in the course of the year. In 1900 Germany's birth rate was 35.6; in 1930 it was 17.6; and in 1939, after six years of Nazi rule, it was 20.4.

When the Nazis came into power the birth-rate in Germany was falling. Big families were out of fashion. The Nazis' aim was to reverse this trend and to persuade Germans to have more children. They used a variety of methods to further this objective.

- Financial incentives to have children were offered. Under the Marriage Loan Scheme, introduced in 1933, couples planning to marry could apply for a loan of up to 1,000 marks, which was payable if the woman agreed to give up her job when the marriage took place. The amount of money to be repaid was then reduced by one-quarter for each child the couple produced.

- There was a massive propaganda campaign to glorify motherhood. At its centre was an honours system which rewarded women who produced large numbers of children. This system was built around the award of the Mother Cross. The Mother Cross was awarded in gold (eight children), silver (six children) or bronze (four children).

- In 1927 a law had been passed which legalised abortion if the life of the mother was in danger. The Nazis scrapped this law in 1933, effectively making it impossible for 'genetically fit' women to get a legal abortion. They also closed birth control clinics. In 1938 they relaxed the divorce laws to encourage remarriage and second families.

- The main Nazi organisation for women, the *Deutsches Frauenwerk* headed by **Gertrud Schlotz-Klink**, offered training courses in the skills of motherhood. Millions of women attended these courses in the 1930s and early 1940s.

## How much impact did Nazi policies towards women have?

Nazi efforts to raise **Germany's birth rate** had only limited success. The birth rate increased a little in the 1930s but it remained well below pre-1914 levels. Nor can it be assumed that this increase was the result of the Nazis' 'pronatalist' policies. It probably had more to do with the improving economic climate. Nazi propaganda glorifying motherhood does not appear to have had much impact. Most of the couples who received money under the Marriage Loan Scheme, for example, did not go on to have large families.

Also unsuccessful were Nazi efforts to persuade women to leave paid work in order to concentrate on the 'little world' of home and family. The percentage of German women engaged in paid work actually rose slightly in the 1930s. The idea that the Nazis forced millions of women out of employment in the 1930s is a myth. What is true is that women found it increasingly hard to win promotion to supervisory and management positions.

In the later 1930s the Nazi regime did an about-turn in its attitude to women and paid work. The introduction of compulsory military service and the expansion of the armed forces left gaps in the industrial workforce which needed to be filled. Women were now told that it was their duty to serve the nation by working in its factories rather than by staying at home and looking after their children.

# Education in Nazi Germany

## What were the Nazis' educational priorities?

The Nazis had two main educational priorities. One was to turn young people into committed Nazis. The other was to prepare young men for military service. A lesser priority was to prepare girls to fulfil their duties as wives and mothers. There was no place at all for the idea that education should be about the development of such qualities as independence of mind and a capacity for critical thought. The Nazis regarded academic study of this kind as worthless.

## How did the school curriculum change under the Nazis?

When the Nazis first came into power they dismissed teachers who were Jews or who were seen as politically unreliable. This purge of the teaching profession did not, however, affect very many people. Most of Germany's teachers were either not opposed to the Nazi regime or were active supporters of it.

The Nazis made big changes to the curriculum taught in schools (see table). Subjects such as mathematics, physics, chemistry, foreign languages and religious education were given fewer slots on the timetable. The subjects which gained at their expense were biology, history and physical education. These were the school subjects to which the Nazis attached most importance. Biology and history were in different ways used for the purpose of **indoctrination**. Physical education was regarded as important because it helped prepare boys for military service and girls for motherhood.

> **Hitler, speaking in 1935**
>
> 'What we look for from our German youth is different from what people wanted in the past. The German youth of the future must be slim and slender, swift as the greyhound, tough as leather, and hard as steel.'

> **Glossary**
>
> **Indoctrination**
>
> This is the process of getting someone to believe something so completely that nothing will shake that belief.

| History | Only German history was taught. The study of pre-20th-century history concentrated on the exploits of great German heroes. Studies in 20th-century history focused on the alleged role of Jews and Communists in bringing about Germany's defeat in the 1914–1918 war and on the 'national revival' brought about by Hitler. |
|---|---|
| Biology | Biology was repackaged as 'racial science'. Students were taught about Nazi race theory, including the alleged differences between 'Aryans' and 'sub-human' Slavs. They were also taught about 'racial hygiene' – in other words, the need for selective breeding. 'Racial hygiene' covered the importance of preventing the 'genetically defective', such as disabled and mentally ill people, from breeding as well as the need for 'Aryans' to have children only with fellow 'Aryans'. |
| Physical Education | Hitler's obsession with promoting physical fitness resulted in the amount of time allocated to physical education being increased to two hours per day. Boys concentrated on cross-country running and on competitive sports: boxing became compulsory. Girls concentrated on gymnastics and dance. |

Teaching in history, biology and physical education in the Nazi era

Other school subjects also made their contribution to the process of indoctrination. Prominent in the chemistry syllabus, for example, were such topics as poisonous gases and explosive materials. In mathematics, students were required to solve problems relating to such matters as the impact of bombing and the cost to the state of the disabled. The idea was to encourage students to be ruthless and pitiless in order to prepare them for Hitler's 'eternal struggle'.

One effect of the Nazi curriculum was a decline in educational standards. By 1939 employers and parents were complaining about falling levels of literacy and numeracy. Nazi leaders were unconcerned. All that mattered in their view was whether students were coming out of school filled with what they called 'the National Socialist spirit'.

## Elite schools

The Nazis did not rely on the mainstream educational system to produce future generations of leaders. They set up elite schools for this purpose. National Political Educational Institutions ('Napolas') were established to prepare students for leadership roles in the civil service and the army. By 1939 16 Napolas were in existence. There were so-called 'Adolf Hitler Schools' as well whose function was to train future Nazi Party leaders. The best graduates of the 'Adolf Hitler Schools' went on to further study at three 'Order Castles'. These were universities of Nazism.

# Youth movements

## The Hitler Youth

The non-Nazi household represented a serious obstacle to Nazi plans to capture the hearts and minds of German young people. In Communist, Social Democratic or Catholic homes children would hear their parents criticising or ridiculing the ideas and values of National Socialism. The Nazis therefore set out to limit the amount of time children spent in the company of such parents. The instrument they developed for this purpose was the Hitler Youth movement. The Hitler Youth organised activities for young people in the evenings and at weekends. In the Hitler Youth young people were fed a diet of Nazi propaganda and were kept away from the potentially harmful influence of their parents.

The Hitler Youth was the only legal youth movement in Nazi Germany. The youth wings of the Weimar political parties were banned in 1933. Youth organisations linked with the Christian churches were disbanded in the mid-1930s. By 1936 the Hitler Youth movement had four million members. At its head was **Baldur von Schirach**. In 1936 the Law on the Hitler Youth was passed. This made membership of the Hitler Youth more or less compulsory.

Young Germans served in the Hitler Youth between the ages of 10 and 18. There were separate organisations for boys and girls, and for different age groups.

| Age | Boys | Girls |
|---|---|---|
| 6–10 | 'Little Fellows' (*Pimpfen*) | |
| 10–14 | German Young People (*Deutsches Jungvolk*) | League of Young Girls (*Jungmädelbund*) |
| 14–18 | Hitler Youth (*Hitler Jugend*) | League of German Girls (*Bund Deutscher Mädel*) |

Organisation of the Hitler Youth movement

## Biography

### Baldur von Schirach (1907–1974)

Von Schirach was the son of an upper-class German father and a wealthy American mother. He was energetic, capable and devoted to Hitler, but his youth and privileged background set him apart from some of the Nazi Party's other top leaders. In 1941 his enemies within the Party succeeded in having him removed from his post as Reich Youth Leader. Between 1941 and 1945 he served as *Gauleiter* of Vienna.

The activities undertaken by boys and girls in the Hitler Youth were in some respects the same. Both attended political education classes. Both did a great deal of physical exercise in the form of hiking, athletics and gymnastics. There were, however, some differences. Boys did a lot of military training – parade-ground drill, map reading, rifle shooting – while girls received training in nursing, child care and household management.

## Did the Nazis' youth policies achieve their objectives?

- There is a quite a lot of evidence which suggests that in the early years of Nazi rule the Hitler Youth was popular among many young Germans. For some the weekend camps were an enjoyable novelty. Others liked the opportunities the Hitler Youth offered to mix with other teenagers.

- Towards the end of the 1930s young people's enthusiasm for the Hitler Youth seems to have waned. There was little variation in the programme of activities. Boredom set in. Political education lectures and parade-ground drill appear to have been especially unpopular. The number of young people absenting themselves from meetings increased.

- A minority of young Germans became rebellious rather than merely apathetic. In Hamburg and Berlin groups of so-called 'Swing Kids' rejected the Hitler Youth in favour of American jazz – a dangerous enthusiasm, because the Nazi authorities regarded jazz as 'degenerate'. The Nazis launched major crackdowns on 'Swing Kids' in 1941 and 1942. More political than the 'Swing Kids' were the 'Edelweiss Pirates', a loose alliance of youth gangs which first appeared in western Germany in the late 1930s. The 'Edelweiss Pirates' disliked the regimented nature of the Hitler Youth. One of their slogans was 'Eternal War on the Hitler Youth'. They made it their business to ambush Hitler Youth patrols and beat up Hitler Youth members. As with the 'Swing Kids', the Nazi regime reacted harshly. Some 'Edelweiss Pirates' had their heads shaved to humiliate them: others were sent to concentration camps.

- There is some evidence which suggests that the relentless emphasis in schools and in the Hitler Youth on the need to be tough and hard had its effect. Some observers in the late 1930s were to be found complaining about the aggressive behaviour of some young Germans. It may not be a coincidence that many of the German soldiers who committed war crimes in Poland and Russia in the 1939–1945 war were drawn from the generation which grew to adulthood in the 1930s.

## Conclusion: how successful were Nazi policies towards women and the young?

Nazi policies towards women and the young aimed not only to influence the ways in which individuals behaved but also the ways in which they thought. Success here was difficult to achieve. Abolishing or Nazifying institutions was straightforward by comparison. Nazi policies towards women largely failed to achieve the desired results. Their policies towards the young may have had more success but certainly did not turn all young Germans into enthusiastic Nazis.

---

### Taking it further

Chapters 3–5 of Lisa Pine, *Hitler's 'National Community': Society and Culture in Nazi Germany* (2007) deal with education, youth groups and women and the family. A study of these chapters would enable you to understand in more detail the similarities and differences in the treatment of boys and girls in Nazi Germany.

---

## Activity: Nazi policies towards women and the young

- After 1933 the Social Democrat Party's leaders living in exile produced a newspaper which aimed to expose the evils of Nazi rule in Germany. Write a brief article of the kind which might have appeared in this newspaper on either the treatment of women or of the young in Nazi Germany.

- 'Nazi policies towards the young were far more effective than their policies towards women.' State how far you would agree with this claim, giving reasons for your answer.

# Chapter 10   The Nazi economy, 1933–1939

## Key questions

- How did the Nazis bring down the level of unemployment in Germany?
- How much credit should be given to the Nazis for bringing down unemployment?
- What did the Nazis mean by a 'war economy'?
- To what extent did the Four Year Plan achieve its objectives?

Hitler had no technical knowledge of economics. As Germany's ruler he made no attempt to involve himself in the details of economic policy. In the economic field he confined himself to making it clear what he wanted to happen. He then left it to others to work out how his wishes were to be met. When he came to power Hitler had two economic objectives, one short-term and the other longer-term. The short-term objective was to bring down the level of unemployment in Germany. Here Hitler's personal prestige and reputation were at stake. At the start of the 1933 election campaign he had promised 'a massive and comprehensive attack on unemployment' which would solve the problem within four years. Failure to deliver on this promise would have left him looking dishonest and incompetent. Hitler's longer-term objective was to reshape Germany's economy as a 'war economy' (*Wehrwirtschaft*). At times Hitler gave the impression that his priority was the prosperity and well-being of the German people. It was not. What he wanted above all was an economy which would enable him to wage total war.

| Timeline | |
|---|---|
| **1933** | Opening of the 'Battle for Work' |
| **1934** | Schacht's 'New Plan' |
| **1936** | Launching of the 'Four Year Plan' under Goering's direction |
| **1937** | Schacht's resignation as Minister of Economics |

## Eliminating unemployment, 1933–1936

### The 'Battle for Work'

The Nazis called their campaign against unemployment the 'Battle for Work'. To mastermind this campaign Hitler brought in **Hjalmar Schacht**. Schacht was appointed chief of Germany's national bank in 1933 and Minister of Economics in 1934. As Minister of Economics he was given very extensive powers. Hitler's decision to make a non-Nazi his economic supremo did not go down well with some of his fellow-Nazis.

When Hitler became Chancellor in January 1933 the number of Germans out of work according to official figures was 5 million. The official figures almost certainly underestimated the level of unemployment: the true figure was probably well over seven million. Over the next five years unemployment fell more quickly in Germany than in any other industrialised country in the world.

## Biography

### Hjalmar Schacht
(1877–1970)

Schacht was Germany's inter-war financial wizard. In 1923 he played a key role in stabilising Germany's currency. He was then made president of Germany's national bank, a post he held until 1930 when he resigned in protest against the final version of the Young Plan. He was reappointed to this post by Hitler in 1933. In the early 1930s Schacht was an admirer of Hitler but he never joined the Nazi Party. He resigned as Minister of Economics in 1937 following policy disagreements with Hitler but he remained a member of the government. From the late 1930s onwards he became increasingly disillusioned with Nazism and in 1944 was arrested and sent to a concentration camp on suspicion of involvement in a plot to kill Hitler.

### Take note

For the periods 1933–1936 and 1936–1939, (i) name the key personality in the management of the German economy, (ii) explain what the main aim of economic policy was in the period in question and (iii) judge the extent to which the main aim was achieved.

|  | Number of unemployed in millions (yearly average) | The % of workforce unemployed (yearly average) |
|---|---|---|
| 1933 | 4.8 | 25.9% |
| 1934 | 2.7 | 13.5% |
| 1935 | 2.1 | 10.3% |
| 1936 | 1.6 | 7.4% |
| 1937 | 0.9 | 4.1% |
| 1938 | 0.4 | 1.9% |
| 1939 | 0.1 | 0.5% |

The unemployed in Germany, 1933–1939 (T. Kirk, 1995)

## How was unemployment brought down?

There was no one single reason for the fall in unemployment in Germany in the years after 1933. There was a variety of factors at work.

- In 1932–1933 the world economic depression bottomed out. In Germany and elsewhere, consumer spending and investment by companies began to pick up. This led to a 'natural' economic recovery – 'natural' in the sense that it was not the result of government policies. The unemployment total in Germany would have come down to some extent even if Hitler's government had done nothing. In Britain in the early 1930s governments did little to fight the slump but the British economy nevertheless started to recover.

- Under Schacht there was substantial investment in a programme of public works. The most eye-catching feature of this programme was the construction of several thousand kilometres of motorway-style roads (*Autobahnen*). These roads became known as 'Adolf Hitler's highways'. Nazi propaganda claimed that building the *Autobahnen* made an important contribution to the reduction of unemployment but the number of jobs created was not in fact very large. Lower-profile job creation schemes involving things like land reclamation, road repairs and house building employed a lot more workers than the building of the *Autobahnen*.

- The government began to rearm. It started to place large orders for warplanes, tanks, trucks and munitions. Airfields were rebuilt and barracks constructed. The Treaty of Versailles, which had imposed severe restrictions on Germany's armed forces, was ignored. A clash with Britain and France was avoided by a cover-up of the scale of German rearmament. The cover-up was organised by Schacht. He kept military spending off the government's published accounts in 1933–1935 by paying arms manufacturers not with money but with 'mefo bills'. 'Mefo bills' were secret government credit notes which manufacturers could then cash at the national bank.

The unemployment statistics were doctored in a number of ways. Jews who were dismissed from their jobs were not counted as unemployed. Nor were women who gave up their jobs under the 1933 Marriage Loan Scheme. A sizeable number of young people were taken off the unemployment register in 1935 when it was decreed that all 19–25 year olds had to do six months' unpaid work in the newly formed Reich Labour Service. In the same year Hitler went public on German rearmament and reintroduced compulsory military service. Compulsory military service contributed to a reduction in the jobless total though clearly this was not the main reason for its reintroduction.

## Schacht's 'New Plan', 1934

The 'Battle for Work' caused problems as well as solving them. The secret rearmament programme sucked huge quantities of imported raw materials into Germany at a time when the country's exporters were struggling due to the taxes on imports, or tariffs, which many countries introduced in the 1930s to protect their industries from foreign competition. This left Germany with a sizeable **trade deficit.** Schacht's response was the so-called 'New Plan' of 1934 under which no one could import goods into Germany without permission from the Ministry of Economics. The 'New Plan' solved the immediate problem but it was bad news for ordinary Germans: it meant fewer food imports and food shortages.

## Did Germany experience an 'economic miracle' after 1933?

In the mid-1930s Nazi propaganda heaped praise on Hitler for conquering unemployment. Many Germans at the time appear to have believed that this praise was deserved. Some later commentators have taken the same view. It is sometimes suggested that the years after 1933 saw a Hitler-inspired 'economic miracle' based on job-creation schemes – schemes of a kind that Brüning and others had been too timid and unimaginative to introduce before 1933. Such suggestions should be treated with caution. Certainly, Nazi job-creation schemes played some part in bringing down unemployment, especially in 1933–1934. But the fall in the number of jobless owed a lot more to 'natural' recovery and to secret rearmament than it did to public-works programmes. Nor did ordinary people see many signs of an 'economic miracle' in their day-to-day lives. The return to full employment did not lead to big improvements in standards of living. Workers in Nazi Germany were badly paid, heavily taxed and were made to work increasingly long hours. They were not as well off as they had been in the 1920s.

# The Nazi 'war economy'

## The Four-Year Plan

By 1936 Hitler had achieved many of his initial goals: the Communists and Social Democrats had been crushed; German institutions had been Nazified; and the 'Battle for Work' had been won. In these circumstances Hitler's thoughts turned to the project closest to his heart: waging war.

**Take note**

Which sections of the community in Germany gained, and which suffered, as a result of Nazi economic policy between 1933 and 1939?

**Glossary**

**Trade deficit**

A country has a trade deficit if the value of what it imports exceeds the value of what it exports. A prolonged trade deficit means that a country goes into debt, something which can have damaging economic effects.

**Take note**

As you work through this chapter, make notes on the impact of Nazi economic policies on the living standards of ordinary Germans using the following as sub-headings: job opportunities, wage levels and the availability of foodstuffs.

**Biography**

## Hermann Goering
(1893–1946)

In the 1930s Goering was effectively Hitler's second-in-command. He had a privileged upbringing and won fame as a fighter pilot in the 1914–1918 war. Goering was a colourful figure whose evident zest for life made him one of the more popular Nazi leaders, but he was also corrupt and enormously vain. He became Commander-in-Chief of the *Luftwaffe*, Germany's air force, when rearmament was announced in 1935 and held this post alongside his responsibilities for the Four-Year Plan.

Hermann Goering in 1932

He prepared a memorandum for his closest colleagues arguing that the German economy had to be made ready for war within four years. Soon afterwards, he launched the Four-Year Plan at the 1936 Nuremberg rally.

In his memorandum Hitler recognised that increasing the size and firepower of Germany's armed forces was only one of the challenges involved in preparing for war. Just as important, he maintained, was the need to ensure that Germany could not be starved of vital resources by its enemies. Here, Hitler was mindful of the impact of the British naval blockade on Germany in the 1914–1918 war. The core aim of the Four-Year Plan was therefore to make Germany's economy as self-sufficient as possible. The technical term used to describe a state of economic self-sufficiency is autarky.

Schacht was alarmed by the Four-Year Plan. He thought Hitler was going too far and too fast. He wanted the pace of rearmament to be slowed. Hitler brushed his objections aside. Schacht's influence waned. He resigned as Minister of Economics in 1937 though he remained a member of the government. Responsibility for implementing the Four-Year Plan was given to **Hermann Goering**. The title he was given was Plenipotentiary for the Four-Year Plan. Goering had no real expertise in economics but he was ambitious, forceful and determined.

### How did Goering try to bring about economic self-sufficiency?

Early twentieth-century Germany was reliant on foreign imports in two main ways. It had to bring in some of the food it consumed from abroad and its industries depended heavily on imported raw materials. Goering therefore aimed to reduce the need for imports of food and raw materials. He tried to do this in a number of ways:

- Attempts were made to encourage German farmers to grow more food. They were, for example, given grants to bring new land under cultivation.

- Industries were required wherever possible to use raw materials available in Germany – even if imported raw materials were cheaper or of better quality. Low-grade home-produced iron ore, for example, was used in preference to higher-quality imported ores.

- There was a huge amount of investment in efforts to develop artificial substitutes for natural products. In German these synthetic products were called *ersatz* goods, meaning artificial or replacement goods. The biggest Four-Year Plan project of all involved building plants to derive motor fuel from coal. Germany had plenty of coal but no oil of its own. There was also heavy investment in *ersatz* rubber.

- An extensive programme of labour retraining was started to ensure that Germany did not run short of workers with essential skills.

## Goering and big business

Goering expected major German companies to co-operate with him. If they did so they were allowed to make big profits. The most notorious example of a company which was only too willing to co-operate with the Nazis was I.G. Farben, the chemicals giant. I.G. Farben was given contracts to produce both synthetic motor fuel and synthetic rubber. It later supplied the Nazi regime with Zyklon-B, the poison gas used to kill prisoners at Auschwitz and other extermination camps.

When big companies failed to co-operate with him, Goering by-passed them and set up state-run industrial facilities. In 1937, for example, the Ruhr iron and steel companies refused to invest in expensive new blast furnaces capable of using low-grade German iron ore. Goering's response was to build a state-owned steelworks called the Hermann Goering Works. By 1940 the Herman Goering Works had developed into a gigantic industrial corporation employing 600,000 people. It branched out from steel making into other activities such as coal mining and armaments manufacture.

# How successful was the Four-Year Plan?

- Hitler did not expect the Four-Year Plan to make Germany self-sufficient in all respects. He knew that this was not possible. He accepted, for example, that Germany was incapable of feeding itself. This was one of the reasons why he claimed that Germany needed 'living space' (*Lebensraum*) in eastern Europe.

- Germany might have been able to grow more of its own food had the Nazi regime not focused on other priorities. Agriculture often had to make way for preparations for war: agricultural labourers were drafted into jobs in armaments factories and land was given over to the armed forces for barracks, camps and airfields. In addition, many agricultural labourers left the land to seek better-paid jobs in the cities. Around 1.4 million workers left the land between 1933 and 1939. This movement away from the land owed something to the Nazis' attempts to reorganise German agriculture. In 1933 the Nazis passed the Reich Entailed Farm Law. This aimed to preserve medium-sized German farms by ensuring that they were passed on to a single heir and not split up among several heirs. One result of the Farm Law was that children who were not heirs had no incentive to remain on the land.

- German steel production increased in the late 1930s but the contribution made to the increase by home-produced iron ore was less than was expected.

- The attempts to produce synthetic materials had mixed success. In 1939 production of synthetic motor fuel was well below the planned level. Synthetic rubber, by contrast, was a success story, with production more or less reaching the targets laid down in the Four-Year Plan (see table below).

- The Four-Year Plan played havoc with Germany's finances. The government ran huge **budget deficits** in the late 1930s. Germany lived beyond its means.

### Glossary

**Budget deficit**

A country has a budget deficit if spending by the government is higher than the government's income from taxation. When a government runs a budget deficit it has to cover it by borrowing money.

**Take note**

Using your own words, write a sentence defining the meaning of each of the following: the 'Battle for Work'; mefo bills; *Autobahnen*; *Wehrwirtschaft*; autarky.

| Commodity | 1936 output | 1938 output | 1942 output | Plan target |
|---|---|---|---|---|
| Motor fuel | 1,790 | 2,340 | 6,260 | 13,380 |
| Synthetic rubber | 0.7 | 5 | 96 | 120 |
| Iron ore | 2,255 | 3,360 | 4,137 | 5,549 |
| Steel | 19,216 | 22,656 | 20,480 | 24,000 |

Output under the Four-Year Plan (measured in thousands of tons (J. Noakes and G. Pridham, 1984)

- In 1939 Germany was still importing more than one-third of its raw material requirements.

- Overall, the Four-Year Plan was only partly successful.

## Conclusion: was Germany ready for war in 1939?

By 1939 Germany had an army of nearly four million men and an air force of 3,000 warplanes. Its military strength had grown out of all recognition since 1933. Germany's army leaders nevertheless doubted whether the country was ready for war. One of their concerns was equipment. The rearmament drive had been hampered by shortages of labour and raw materials. There had also been mismanagement. The result was that the army had not by 1939 been provided with all of the supplies it was expecting. Stocks of ammunition, for example, were low and much of the army was still reliant on horse-drawn transport. The other main concern of the army leaders was the possibility of a long war against several enemies. They did not believe that Germany had the underlying economic strength needed to fight a war similar to that of 1914–1918. Germany's main weakness, they argued, was the lack of guaranteed supplies of essential raw materials. The worst problem was oil. Hitler reacted with impatience to the worries expressed by his army chiefs in the late 1930s. In 1938 he sacked Germany's two leading generals, Blomberg and Fritsch, and took personal command of Germany's armed forces. Events, however, were to prove his generals right.

**Taking it further**

If you want to find out more about the Nazi economy, there is illuminating material in the online resource *German History in Documents and Images* (GDHI). In the document collection on *Nazi Germany 1933–1945* edited by Richard Breitman, find Hitler's analysis of Germany's economic strengths and weaknesses in his 1936 memorandum on autarky and the report of the Social Democratic Party in exile on the mood of Germany's workers in 1938.

## Activity: Nazi economic policy, 1933–1939

- 'The Nazis should not be credited with success in the "Battle for Work" because all they did was manipulate the unemployment figures.' How far do you agree with this view?

- 'Among the positive achievements of Hitler the one outshining all others was his economic miracle.' This claim was made in 1979 by the respected German writer Sebastian Haffner. What reasons could be advanced (i) in support of and (ii) in opposition to this claim? On balance, would you accept Haffner's claim?

- 'By 1939 the cracks in an economy which was operating beyond its capacity were beginning to show.' What arguments can be offered in support of this suggestion?

# Skills Builder 3: **Writing introductions and conclusions**

When answering questions in Unit 1, students will be expected to write an essay. So far, in Skills Builder 1, you have learned the importance of writing in paragraphs and, in Skills Builder 2, you have learned about the importance of showing a clear argument when answering questions on causation and change.

In this third Skills Builder, we will be looking at the importance of writing introductory and concluding paragraphs.

In the exam, you should spend approximately 40 minutes on your whole essay, including:

- planning what you are going to write
- writing a separate paragraph for each major point you wish to make
- checking what you have written.

Therefore, given the time constraints, you should not spend more than five minutes writing your introduction.

## **What should you put in your introduction?**

Your introduction should set out what you plan to cover and discuss in your essay answer. Your introduction needs to show that you will answer the question in an analytical way – and that you haven't just started writing without thinking. Therefore, it is good to say, very briefly, what you are going to argue in the essay. You can then refer back to your introduction as you write to make sure that your argument is on track.

We are going to look at an introduction to an answer to the following question:

> (A) How successful was Nazi economic policy in achieving prosperity within Germany by 1939?

This question asks you to make a judgment about the success of Nazi economic policy – not in preparing Germany for war, but in making the country prosperous.

The question will require you to consider ways in which Nazi policy brought about prosperity (the reduction of unemployment) and ways in which it did not (food shortages, high taxes, low pay, longer hours of work). You then need to make a judgment about whether any gains in prosperity were outweighed by losses.

Here is an example of an introduction you might write.

*Nazi economic policy between 1933 and 1939 was successful to some degree in achieving prosperity within Germany, but it cannot be said that the Nazis presided over an 'economic miracle' which meant that ordinary Germans were much better off in 1939 than they had been in the 1920s. Two main points will be made in this essay. First, it will be argued that Nazi economic policy contributed to the return of full employment and therefore brought some measure of prosperity to Germany. Second, it will be suggested that Nazi economic policy had the effect of forcing down living standards, leaving many Germans less well off than they had been before the slump.*

This introduction answers the question directly. It offers a clear judgment on the extent to which Nazi economic policy had brought about prosperity by 1939, and it indicates what is going to be argued in the main body of the essay which will follow.

# Activity: Spot the mistake

The following introductions have been written in response to the question above. Each one illustrates a common mistake. Spot them!

## Example 1

When the Nazis came into power in 1933 the German economy was in a terrible state. More than 25 percent of the workforce was unemployed. The Nazis promised to put Germany back to work and to win what they called 'the Battle for Work'. By 1936 unemployment had been more or less completely eliminated and prosperity had returned to Germany.

## Example 2

Nazi economic policy after 1933 had two main aims. One was to reduce unemployment and the other was to prepare Germany to fight wars against its enemies. In the early years of Nazi rule it was the reduction of unemployment which took priority, but after 1936 the Nazis concentrated their efforts on building a 'war economy'. Building a war economy was the main economic aim of the Nazis. The prosperity of the German people took second place behind preparing for war.

## Example 3

The main way in which the Nazis had brought about prosperity by 1939 was by returning the country to full employment. The Nazis reduced unemployment by using a variety of methods. One was through their public works programme, the centrepiece of which was the building of motorways or autobahnen. The Nazis built these high-quality roads partly for military reasons. Another way in which the Nazis reduced unemployment was through secret rearmament, which they financed by means of 'mefo-bills'. Lastly, the Nazis reduced unemployment by cooking the books. For example, Jews who were forced out of work were not included in the unemployment figures.

## Answers

Example 1 – this introduction identifies a way in which Nazi economic policy brought about prosperity, but it suggests that this is the only point which is going to be considered and that the essay which follows is not going to offer a balanced discussion of ways in which Nazi policy promoted prosperity and ways in which it did not.

Example 2 – this introduction does not focus tightly on the question set, but instead considers the various aims of Nazi economic policy and their relative importance.

Example 3 – among other things, this introduction makes one of the most common mistakes of all, that of including within it points and evidence which belong in the main body of the essay and not in its introductory paragraph.

It is important that your essay does not contradict your introduction. If you suggest in your introduction that Nazi economic policy was not entirely successful in bringing about prosperity, then you must maintain this argument throughout your essay.

## Introduction: DOs and DON'Ts

- DO look at the question and decide your line of argument.
- DO make reference to the question in your introduction.
- DO show what you intend to argue.
- DON'T begin your answer by writing a story.
- DON'T spend too long writing your introduction. Five minutes is enough.

## Activity: Write your own introduction

Write an introduction to the following question:

(B) How accurate is it to say that the persecution of the Jews in Germany steadily intensified in the years 1933–1942?

## Why are conclusions important?

When you are asked a question in an examination, you are expected to answer it! The concluding paragraph is very important in this process. It should summarise the argument you have made, with your verdict on the question. It should not be more than three or four sentences in length, and under examination conditions it should take no more than five minutes to write.

Here is an example conclusion for Question (A).

Nazi economic policy had certainly not been completely successful by 1939 in achieving prosperity in Germany. It is true that many Germans who had been jobless in 1933 had been put back to work by 1939. No doubt they recognised that their position in the late 1930s was not as bad as it had been in 1933. However, full employment does not necessarily mean prosperity. Standards of living in Germany in 1939 were in general lower than they had been in the 1920s.

## Activity: Write your own conclusion

Using Question (B) above, write a conclusion of not more than four sentences. Try to write it in five minutes.

## Activity: Write an introduction and a conclusion

Here is another example of a question:

(C) Why did the Nazis after 1933 attach so much importance to their policies towards women and young people?

**Tip – plan the conclusion first.** You will always find it easier to write an introduction once you have decided what your conclusion will be. This is because, once you know where your answer is going, you can introduce it.

# Chapter 11   Germany at war, 1939–1945

## Key questions

- How was the German economy organised in wartime?
- What impact did the Allied bombing campaign have on Germany?
- What was the condition of Germany in 1945?
- Why did Germany lose the 1939–1945 war?

In 1939 Hitler gave a speech to his army chiefs in which he listed Germany's strengths. He started with himself. 'No one will ever again have the confidence of the whole German people as I do', he declared. Hitler's claim was no doubt arrogant. But it was not wildly inaccurate. Hitler enjoyed widespread popularity in Germany in the 1930s. His popularity owed a lot to what he had done within the country. It owed maybe even more to his foreign policy. In 1935–1936 he defied the Versailles Treaty – first when he announced German rearmament and then when he sent the German army back into the Rhineland. Next he turned his attention to the task of creating a 'greater Germany' which contained within its borders all of the German-speaking people in Europe. In early 1938 his native Austria became part of Germany. Later in 1938 Czechoslovakia was arm-twisted into handing over to Germany its German-speaking province known as the Sudetenland. These foreign policy successes were loudly applauded by the German people. Hitler went on to become more reckless and aggressive. In 1939 his demand for the return of the 'Polish corridor' led to war with Poland and its allies, Britain and France. In mid-1941 he launched his war of conquest against the Soviet Union. And in December 1941 he declared war on the United States after his ally, Japan, had attacked Pearl Harbor. Hitler's aggressiveness was not only to cost him his popularity in Germany and to bring about his downfall. It was also to bring ruin on his people.

| Timeline | |
|------|------|
| **1939** | German invasion of Poland |
| **1941** | Operation Barbarossa launched; USA's entry into the war |
| **1942** | Speer appointed Armaments Minister |
| **1943** | German surrender at Stalingrad |
| **1944** | Allied invasion of France |
| **1945** | Invasion of Germany; suicide of Hitler, Goebbels and Himmler |

## War in Europe, 1939–1945: overview

Seen from Germany's point of view, the war in Europe between 1939 and 1945 can be broken down into three phases: a period of conquest (1939–1942); a period of decisive reverses (1942–1943); and a period of retreat (1943–1945).

## Conquest, 1939–1942

In 1939 Germany crushed Poland in a few weeks. In the spring of 1940 it occupied Norway and Denmark. The occupation of Norway was quickly followed by the fall of Holland, Belgium and France in May–June 1940. Hitler then toyed with the idea of crossing the Channel but put his plans to invade Britain on hold after his air force failed to win control of the skies over south-east England. He turned his attention to Russia. In 1940–1941 he prepared the ground for an attack on Soviet Russia by tightening his grip on south-eastern Europe. Hungary, Romania and Bulgaria became Germany's allies and Yugoslavia and Greece were invaded. The attack on Soviet Russia, code-named 'Operation Barbarossa', was launched in June 1941. Huge tracts of western Russia fell to the Nazis in the first year of fighting. In early 1942 Hitler was at the height of his power.

## Decisive reverses, 1942–1943

In 1942–1943 the German armies suffered two shattering defeats on the so-called 'Eastern Front'. The first was at **Stalingrad** (August 1942–January 1943) and the second was in the tank battle of **Kursk** (July 1943). These two battles forced Germany's armies in Soviet Russia on to the retreat. Meanwhile, in North Africa, German forces were sent to help Mussolini's Italy hold Libya and later attempted to fight their way through to the oil fields of the Middle East. They were defeated by the British at El Alamein (October 1942) and surrendered to British and American forces at Tunis (May 1943). The 'Desert War' – as it was known – diverted German resources away from the Eastern Front.

## Retreat, 1943–1945

On the Eastern Front, Russian armies advanced westwards, entering Poland in mid-1944 and Germany itself in January 1945. In western Europe, Anglo-American forces landed in Normandy in June 1944 and entered German territory in October 1944. There were in this phase of the war some ferocious German counter-attacks which held up both the Russians in the east and the British and Americans in the west. Germany was, however, fighting a losing battle. Hitler committed suicide on 30 April 1945.

# Political developments during the war

### Radicalisation

From the late 1930s onwards Nazi policy became increasingly radical.

- In 1937–1938 Hitler removed non-Nazi conservatives like Schacht from positions of influence in his government because they voiced doubts about his plans to wage war in the near future.

- In 1939 Hitler embarked on the war non-Nazi conservatives had warned him against.

- Under the cover of war, the Nazis launched genocidal policies – not only the Holocaust, but also the mass killing of the Roma and Sinti and of the mentally ill and disabled through the T-4 'euthanasia' programme (see Chapter 8).

### Stalingrad and Kursk

Stalingrad and Kursk were arguably the two most important battles of the Second World War. They were, however, very different in character. At Stalingrad the Germans battled to win control of a built-up area street-by-street and house-by-house before they were themselves surrounded by a Russian counter-attack and forced to surrender. Kursk, by contrast, was a battle fought in open country across a wide area, with tanks at the centre of things. One of the clashes in the battle of Kursk involved hundreds of Russian and German tanks near the small town of Prokhorovka – the biggest tank battle the world has ever seen. The battle of Kursk was a major turning-point in the war in Europe because the Russians stopped a major German attack, codenamed Operation Citadel, and forced the German armies in Russia on to the retreat.

Kursk, 1943

## Hitler's disappearance from public view

After the war began Hitler was seen in public less and less. He spent most of his time at his military headquarters. He did not visit German troops in the battle zones; he did not go to German cities hit by Allied bombing raids to offer comfort to the victims; and he did not try to mobilise support for the war effort by making numerous speeches and radio broadcasts. In the later stages of the war, Propaganda Minister Goebbels replaced Hitler as the public face of the Nazi regime. While Hitler moped at his military headquarters, blaming his generals and even the German people for letting him down, Goebbels criss-crossed Germany encouraging people to fight on.

## Resistance

Resistance to Nazism was limited in the 1930s. In part this was because Hitler was popular, in part because of the effectiveness of Himmler's *Gestapo*, the secret police. By the mid 1930s the *Gestapo* had largely destroyed the underground networks set up in 1933 by two potentially dangerous enemies, the Social Democrats and the Communists. An exception to this record of *Gestapo* effectiveness was the Communist spy ring known as the *Rote Kapelle* ('Red Orchestra'). It managed to survive until 1942, when its leaders were arrested and executed.

The later years of the war saw an increase in resistance to Nazism within Germany. The resisters came from a variety of backgrounds and were inspired by different motives.

- The members of the Communist resistance, which re-emerged in working-class heartlands such as the Ruhr, were old foes of the Nazis.

- The 'White Rose' group based at Munich University consisted of idealistic university students horrified by Nazi anti-Jewish atrocities. Its members distributed anti-Nazi leaflets and daubed the walls of public buildings with anti-Nazi graffiti. Its leaders, among them Hans and Sophie Scholl, were arrested in 1943 and executed.

- The 'Kreisau Circle' was a loose association of upper-class political moderates brought together by a shared loathing of Nazi barbarism. It took its name from its meeting-place – the country estate of Helmuth von Moltke, one of its leaders. The 'Kreisau Circle' was essentially a discussion group which concentrated on drawing up plans for a post-war democratic Germany.

- The 'Beck–Goerdeler' group was made up of old-fashioned upper-class nationalists who turned against Nazism when it became clear that Hitler was leading Germany to defeat and disaster. Its key figures were Ludwig Beck (1880–1944), until 1938 one of the most senior officers in the German army, and Carl Goerdeler (1884–1945), a member of the government in the early years of Nazi rule. Their plan was to remove Hitler from power by assassinating him.

### Taking it further

1. Conduct further research into the 20 July Plot (or 'Operation Valkyrie' as it was known). Try to find out about the scale of the plot and what happened to the plotters.

2. Investigate further other wartime resistance movements such as the White Rose, the Red Orchestra and the Kreisau Circle. In each case, try to deepen your understanding of:
   – what kind of people were involved in the movement
   – what they did
   – how successful they were and why.

## The 'July Plot', 1944

Beck and Goerdeler had many supporters in the senior ranks of the German army and so knew they could get close to Hitler. In July 1944 they made their move. One of their supporters, **Claus von Stauffenberg**, planted a bomb in a conference room at Hitler's military headquarters. Four people were killed when it went off but Hitler escaped serious injury. Those connected with the 'July Plot' were executed.

# The German economy in wartime

## The use of foreign resources

The territories which Germany gained during its period of conquest helped it to overcome some of the economic difficulties which it had faced before it went to war.

- Germany gained access to new food supplies and to some key raw materials as a result of its conquests. France provided coal and iron ore, Romania oil and the southern part of Russia wheat. Germany was also able to exploit industrial facilities located within the conquered territories – steelworks and munitions factories in France and Belgium, for example.

- Germany captured large quantities of military equipment which it was able to put to use. Former French tanks and artillery were in service with the German army right up until 1945.

- The conquered territories provided Germany with much-needed supplies of labour. The Nazis put French and Russian prisoners of war to work in their factories. They also transported millions of civilians to Germany from Poland, France and other occupied countries to work as slave labourers. By 1944 there were eight million foreign slave labourers working in Germany. They made up something like one-fifth of the German workforce. These workers were treated atrociously. Companies which made extensive use of slave labour included BMW (motor vehicles), I.G. Farben (chemicals), Messerschmitt (aircraft) and Krupps (munitions). Prisoners held in SS-run concentration and extermination camps were also used as slave labourers. Himmler's SS built up huge business enterprises on the basis of concentration camp labour. There were SS-run firms making things like building materials, clothing, furniture and armaments.

The conquered territories did not, however, meet all of Germany's needs. Most slave labourers were unskilled. The German war effort was hampered throughout by shortages of highly skilled workers such as electricians and aircraft fitters. Oil was also in short supply. Synthetic fuel and the Romanian oilfields could not keep up with demand. Hitler hoped to overcome the oil problem by seizing control of the Baku oilfield in southern Russia. Defeat at Stalingrad in 1943 put paid to his hopes.

**Biography**

### Claus von Stauffenberg
(1907–1944)

Colonel von Stauffenberg belonged to a family of south German Catholic aristocrats. A career soldier, he saw wartime service in France, Russia and North Africa. He received several awards for bravery and was also very seriously wounded. Unable to serve at the battlefront because of his wounds, he was employed as a military planner – a role which brought him into direct contact with Hitler. Von Stauffenberg was not strongly anti-Nazi in the early 1930s, but was sickened by what he saw of the treatment of Jews and other civilians in Russia after 1941.

**Take note**

As you work through this section, (i) summarise the ways in which Germany's economic position improved as a result of its conquests in 1939–1942 and (ii) identify the continuing weaknesses of the Germany economy.

## Albert Speer

### (1905–1981)

Speer joined the Nazi Party as a 26-year-old in 1931. He rose to prominence in the 1930s as Hitler's personal architect and as a member of Hitler's inner circle of friends. In the late 1930s Speer worked on ambitious plans to rebuild Berlin, which Hitler intended to rename 'Germania'. When he was put on trial for war crimes in 1946, Speer unconvincingly tried to present himself as a non-political administrator who knew little about the worst excesses of Nazi rule.

Albert Speer in 1943

### Take note

Using the information in this chapter, explain in your own words the reasons why Germans fought on in 1944–1945, despite the fact that the war appeared lost.

## How did Albert Speer contribute to the German war effort?

In 1942 Hitler made **Albert Speer** his Armaments Minister. The amount of power Speer was given was so extensive that he effectively replaced Goering as Germany's economic supremo. By 1942 Goering's position had been weakened by repeated failure. As head of the German air force, he had failed to stop the British evacuation at Dunkirk in 1940, failed to win the Battle of Britain and then failed to prevent the bombing of German cities. Hitler lost confidence in him.

In some ways Speer was a surprising choice as Armaments Minister. He had no military experience and no background in industry. On the other hand, he was a first-class organiser and a personal friend of Hitler's. He was also a realist. He recognised that the era of quick German victories won by *Blitzkrieg* ('lightning war') methods was over and saw that Germany had to reorganise itself for prolonged 'total' war.

Speer proved to be highly effective in his new role. Under his direction big increases in armaments production took place. By 1944 weapons production had been trebled. Speer replaced a chaotic system in which different government departments competed against each other for resources with more orderly arrangements. He tried to concentrate production in a small number of gigantic factories. He streamlined production, cutting out waste and duplication. Ineffective managers were sacked. More intensive use was made of foreign slave labour. Speer's task, however, became increasingly difficult, mainly as a result of the damage inflicted from 1943 onwards by the Anglo-American bombing campaign. Overall, his efforts enabled Germany to hold out for longer than it might otherwise have done but he could not prevent defeat.

## The impact of war on German society

### Military casualties

The human cost of war was immense. Between 1939 and 1945 16 million men served in the ranks of the German army. Over 3 million of them were killed in action and 1.5 million were taken prisoner. Most of those taken prisoner by the Russians died in captivity. Casualty rates increased as the war approached its end. More German soldiers died in the last four months of the war than in the previous two years combined.

| Year | Number |
|------|--------|
| 1939–1940 | 0.09 million |
| 1940–1941 | 0.16 million |
| 1941–1942 | 0.49 million |
| 1942–1943 | 0.47 million |
| 1943–1944 | 0.57 million |
| 1945 | 1.47 million |

German military deaths, 1939–1945 (T. Kirk, 1995)

The later stages of the war saw desperate measures being taken to keep Germany's enemies at bay. In 1944 Hitler ordered the creation of a 'People's Army' (*Volkssturm*), a sort of home guard made up of men aged 16–60 who were not in the armed forces. Members of the Hitler Youth were also pressed into service. Some of those who fought in the defence of Berlin in 1945 were as young as 14.

## Bombing and its effects

Between 1943 and 1945 Germany came under intense attack from the air. The Americans bombed by day and the British by night. The impact of this air assault on those living in Germany was devastating. Despite the fact that Germany had a well-organised air defence system, over 300,000 civilians were killed and 750,000 were injured. Over one-fifth of Germany's housing stock was damaged or destroyed. At the end of the war over seven million Germans were homeless. The centres of Germany's main cities had been reduced to rubble.

| Hamburg | 75% |
|---------|-----|
| Cologne | 61% |
| Stuttgart | 56% |
| Frankfurt | 52% |
| Munich | 42% |
| Berlin | 33% |

Percentage (%) of the built-up area of major German cities destroyed by Allied bombing (R. Overy, 1996)

One of the aims of British and American air raids was to damage the German war economy. This made the Ruhr area a particularly inviting target. It was attacked repeatedly by the Royal Air Force. But the air assault was also designed to cause panic and break civilian morale. This was the intention behind two of the most controversial air raids of the war, the firebombing of Hamburg (July 1943) and of Dresden (February 1945). These two raids alone cost at least 60,000 people their lives. In the face of this onslaught from the air the German people displayed considerable resilience. The authorities organised efficient clear-up operations, which helped to sustain morale. Only in the last months of the war did people lose the will to fight on. However, the bombing campaign meant that from 1943 onwards millions of Germans lived in fear and misery.

### Taking it further

The figures given here for German military and civilian casualties are estimates. Try to confirm their accuracy by doing an online search using search terms like 'German casualties in the Second World War'. If you discover sources which give figures different from those given in this chapter, how would you account for the difference? Why is it so hard to be certain about casualty figures? Investigate German losses of men and materials in the key battles of Stalingrad, Kursk and El Alamein and evaluate their impact on the course of the war.

Dresden, 1945

## Refugees

The German armies which invaded Soviet Russia in 1941 treated the civilian population in a ruthless and savage manner. Atrocities occurred routinely and on a large scale. The same thing happened when Russian troops entered the eastern districts of Germany in 1945. Terrified of the Soviet army, German civilians in these areas fled westwards. Between January and May 1945 some five million Germans left their homes. Since eastern Germany remained under Communist control at the end of the war, few of them ever returned. The authorities in western Germany were left to deal with huge numbers of displaced people.

## German women at war

| | |
|------|------|
| 1940 | 41% |
| 1941 | 43% |
| 1942 | 46% |
| 1943 | 49% |
| 1944 | 51% |

Percentage (%) of Germany's civilian workforce who were women (excludes foreign labourers) (C. Macnab, 2009)

With so many men away serving in the army, the burden of keeping families together and maintaining some semblance of normality fell heavily on German women. The difficulties facing them were immense. Not only were air raids an ever-present danger, but food, clothing and fuel were strictly rationed. Women were also expected wherever possible to make a contribution to the war effort by working in factories or on the land. The war years did not, however, see a spectacular increase in the number of women involved in paid employment. This was because the number of women working in industry or agriculture was very high even before war broke out.

### From a Gestapo report on public opinion in Berlin, July 1943

'Since Stalingrad the telling of nasty jokes about the person of the *Führer* has increased significantly. There is widespread enthusiasm for criticising the Party leadership. The use of the German salute (*Heil Hitler!*) has decreased strikingly in recent months. It has also been noted that many comrades have stopped wearing their Party badges.'

The end of the war brought one final horror for German women. The Soviet soldiers who in 1945 advanced into eastern Germany and captured Berlin engaged in acts of rape on a massive scale. The number of victims in Berlin alone has been estimated at more than 100,000.

## Wartime propaganda

Propaganda minister Goebbels used a number of ploys from 1943 onwards to try to persuade the German people not to give up. He declared that Germany would suffer 'total destruction' if it did not wage 'total war'. He played on people's fears of the Russians, warning of the horrors that would follow a Soviet invasion. He claimed that Germany was developing miracle weapons which would enable it to snatch victory from the jaws of defeat. But Goebbels could not prevent support for the Nazi regime from ebbing away. In 1943–1945 trust in the Nazi regime was unsurprisingly in very steep decline.

# Why did Germany lose the war?

## Economic resources

Between 1941 and 1945 Germany was fighting Britain, Soviet Russia and the United States simultaneously. These were three of the world's most powerful economies. Each of them had access to abundant supplies of raw materials and each of them had huge manufacturing potential. The USA's economy was so strong that it was not only able to supply its own needs but was also able to give vast amounts of aid to its allies. The economic resources available to Germany were nothing like as extensive as those at the disposal of its enemies. It had fewer people, fewer factories and fewer raw materials. The figures for wartime munitions production give some idea of what Germany was up against (see table below). 'This war will be won by industrial production', said the Russian leader, Stalin, in 1941. So it proved. The main reason for Germany's defeat was its inability to match the combined economic resources of Britain, Russia and the USA.

| | Aircraft | Tanks | Artillery pieces |
|---|---|---|---|
| **Britain** | 131 | 30 | 39 |
| **Russia** | 158 | 76 | 224 |
| **USA** | 324 | 105 | 485 |
| **Germany** | 117 | 61 | 94 |

Munitions production of the major powers, 1939–1945 (in thousands) (R. Overy, 2006)

The economic power of Germany's enemies did not, however, mean that the outcome of the war was an entirely foregone conclusion. Countries with strong economies do not automatically have armies which are determined and effective. Britain and France matched Germany in economic strength in 1940 but they fared badly on the battlefield. Remember too that the alliance between Britain, Russia and the United States after 1941 was fragile. Stalin was deeply suspicious of the British and the Americans. Had the alliance broken down, with Stalin making a separate peace with Hitler, the outcome of the war might have been different.

## Effective Allied fighting forces

The German army was a formidable fighting machine throughout the war. In 1939–1941 it won quick and spectacular victories. On the retreat in 1942–1945 it proved stubborn and resilient. It took Germany's enemies time to build up forces of comparable quality. Early defeats at the hands of superior German armies demonstrated to both the British and the Russians just how much ground they had to make up. In their different ways, both turned things around. At the end of the war British and Russian forces were better equipped, better trained and better led than they had been at the start.

> ### Goebbels' 'total war' speech, 18 February 1943
>
> 'Total war is the demand of the hour. The danger facing us is enormous. The efforts we take to meet it must be just as enormous. We can no longer make only partial and careless use of the war potential at home and in the significant parts of Europe that we control. We must use our full resources, as quickly and thoroughly as it is organisationally and practically possible. Everyone knows that if we lose, all will be destroyed.'

The turnaround in Russia was crucial because it was on the Eastern Front that the most decisive battles of the war took place. Russia's military performance in 1941 was utterly disastrous. Huge amounts of territory were lost. So too were four million men, 8,000 aircraft and 17,000 tanks. But lessons were learnt. Changes were made in the Russian army's training, organisation, tactics and leadership. Morale improved. An enormous will to win emerged. Germany's defeat cannot be explained without reference to the fighting qualities displayed by Russian soldiers – and, of course, by their counterparts in the other Allied forces.

## Hitler's miscalculations and mistakes

Hitler was not the only wartime leader to make mistakes. Churchill (UK), Stalin (Soviet Russia) and Roosevelt (USA) made them too. But Hitler made mistakes on an epic scale. Four of them stand out.

- After the fall of Poland and France, Hitler assumed that Britain would make peace and leave him free to attack Russia. He did not allow for Winston Churchill's stubborn determination in 1940 to fight on.

- Hitler massively under-estimated Russia's capacity to wage war. He viewed Russians as racial inferiors and believed they would give up without much of a fight when Germany attacked. 'We only have to kick in the front door and the whole rotten structure will collapse', he told his subordinates before 'Operation Barbarossa' was launched in mid-1941.

- In late 1941 Hitler abruptly declared war on the United States. He did so a few days after the Japanese attack on the Americans at Pearl Harbor. Hitler was relaxed about this decision. He seems to have believed that the US would come to Britain's aid sooner or later whatever he did. He also believed that it would be years before the US could mobilise its economic resources against him. In fact, Hitler's decision was a momentous one. Although it was Japanese aggression that had involved them in war, the Americans opted to make the defeat of Germany their first priority. In addition, the American 'genius for mass production', as Roosevelt called it, made itself felt far more quickly than Hitler expected.

- The 250,000-strong German army which found itself besieged at Stalingrad in late 1942 could have fought its way through the encircling Russian forces back to the safety of the German lines. All the military advice Hitler received supported the idea of a 'break-out' of this kind. But he ignored his advisers and ordered his generals in Stalingrad to fight to the last man. Eventually the army in Stalingrad was forced to surrender: 150,000 Germans were killed and 100,000 taken prisoner.

## The bombing of Germany

The Anglo-American air assault on Germany remains controversial. Whether it was legitimate to target civilians is a matter which continues to be hotly debated. In military terms, though, the bombing campaign made a significant contribution to Germany's defeat.

- It cut the output from Germany's factories in the later stages of the war by about 20 percent.

- Germany had to use scarce resources to build new factories in areas less likely to be bombed.

- Germany was forced to use much of its air force to combat the Allied bombers. By 1944 over 80 percent of the *Luftwaffe's* fighter aircraft were being used to defend the skies over Germany. This meant that they were not available to give support to German ground forces in the battle zones. In the summer of 1944, for example, there were only 200 German warplanes facing the 12,000 Allied aircraft involved in the invasion of France.

## Conclusion: why was Germany defeated?

**There were many reasons for Germany's defeat in the 1939–1945 war. Others could be added to those which have been highlighted here. Britain and the United States both benefited from inspirational political leadership in the Second World War. The work of British code-breakers in many cases gave Germany's enemies advanced warning of its intentions. Resistance movements in many European countries tied down large numbers of German soldiers. The list could go on. But three of the causes of Germany's defeat were more important than the others: Germany's relative economic weakness; the success of Germany's enemies in creating highly motivated and effective armed forces; and Hitler's miscalculations.**

## Activity: Debating Germany's defeat in the 1939–1945 war

- Divide into seven groups.

- Allocate each group one of the years 1939–1945. Each group should draw up a list of reasons why the year it has been allocated might be considered to be the one in which Germany's defeat became inevitable. Groups to report back to the whole class with a brief presentation of their reasons. Having heard the presentations, the class should consider whether it can agree on which was the year in which defeat became inevitable, and why.

- 'Hitler's errors were the main reason for Germany's defeat in the 1939–1945 war.' To what extent would you agree with this claim?

### Taking it further

If you want to study further the controversy surrounding the Allied air offensive against Germany, read chapter 4 of Richard Overy (2006) *Why the Allies Won* and chapter 3 of A.C. Grayling (2006) *Among the Dead Cities*. On the basis of your reading, construct a table explaining how the views of Overy and Grayling differ on the impact of the Allied bombing campaign on (i) German war production and (ii) German civilian morale.

# Skills Builder 4: **Extended writing**

So far, in the Skills Builders, you have learned about:

- the importance of writing in paragraphs
- answering questions on causation and change
- how to write introductions and conclusions.

Now you are going to learn how to write a full response to an examination question. Remember, you will only have 40 minutes for each answer so you need to make the most of your time.

**Read the QUESTION PAPER thoroughly**

You will have a choice of two questions on this topic, but you only need to answer one. Make sure you make the right choice. Don't rush, and give yourself a few minutes to decide which question to answer. You won't have time to change your mind halfway through the exam.

**Read YOUR CHOSEN QUESTION thoroughly**

Once you have made your choice, examine the question and work out what you are expected to do.

## What is the question asking you to do?

There are a number of different types of question you could be asked. Examples are:

- How far?
- How important?
- How accurate?
- To what extent?
- Why?

Make sure that your answer is relevant to the type of question that has been asked.

In the first four question types, you will be expected to organise your factual knowledge and understanding of a topic into a 'For' versus 'Against' format, where you weigh up the importance of each factor/reason/point you mention in relation to the question. You will need to reach a judgment on the question in hand. The fifth type, a question beginning 'Why', will expect you to show how the factors combined to bring about an outcome.

In your planning you also need to be clear about the focus of the question. For example, is it asking you to assess the reasons for something, the result of something or the extent to which something has changed?

For instance:

> (A) How far do you agree that the involvement of the United States in the Second World War was the main cause of Germany's defeat?

> (B) How far do you agree that Nazi economic policies in the years 1933–1945 were a failure?

Both these questions begin 'How far...?' but their focus is different. (A) asks you for an assessment of the relative importance of the causes of Germany's defeat in the Second World War, while (B) asks you to make and support a judgment on the success of Nazi economic policies in peace and war.

## Make a plan

Once you are clear about what the question is asking, sketch out what you intend to cover. Write down what you think will be relevant information in the form of a bulleted list or a mind map. Then organise your information in a way which best answers the question.

## Writing the answer

Make sure that you:

- Write a brief introduction, setting out your argument and what you will be discussing in your answer.

- Write a separate paragraph for each of the factors or reasons that you discuss. In each paragraph, make sure that you make a clear point and support it with specific examples.

- At the end of each paragraph, make a clear link between the point you have made and the question, showing how the point answers the question.

- Avoid just writing descriptions.

- Avoid merely 'telling the story'.

- Write a concluding paragraph which sums up your argument and provides a clear judgment on the question.

## Pace yourself

Success in an examination is based partly on effective time management. If you have approximately 40 minutes to answer a question, make sure that after about 12 or 13 minutes you have written about one-third of your answer. After 35 minutes you should be thinking about and then writing your conclusion.

If you run short of time, make sure that you still write a proper conclusion. If necessary, you can save time by cutting short your treatment of the paragraph or paragraphs before the conclusion by:

- writing the first sentence containing your point

- bullet-pointing your evidence – the information that backs it up

- writing the last sentence of the paragraph which explains the link between your point and the question.

Read the question paper thoroughly

Be clear about the focus of the question you have chosen

Timing: pace yourself

Make a brief plan of your answer before starting to write

## Activity: Write your own answer

Now write your own answer to this question, following the guidance given above:

(C) How accurate is it to say that Hitler's errors and misjudgments were the main cause of Germany's defeat in the Second World War?

# Examzone

Now that you have finished the course content, you will have to do the last bits of preparation for the exam itself. This advice covers two important elements for exam success: revising the information and using your information well in the examination.

This topic – 'From Second Reich to Third Reich: Germany 1918–45' is part of Edexcel's Option F: The Expansion and Challenge of Nationalism, in Unit 1. The Unit 1 exam will be 1 hour and 20 minutes in length, and is worth 60 marks in total.

In the exam you will be given the choice of two questions on the topic Germany 1918–1945. You will be expected to answer one of these and should spend no more than half the examination time answering it. You will also have to answer another question from a different topic. You will be expected to answer the questions you choose in essay form.

## What to expect

You will need to remember information, but the exam is mainly testing whether or not you can apply the relevant information in answering a question. You will be assessed on your ability to recall and select historical knowledge and to deploy it (i.e. make use of knowledge to support your points). You can see that it's not just knowing what happened which counts, but understanding how to use what you know.

You will also be assessed on your ability to present historical explanations that show an understanding of history. You should read the question carefully to make sure you answer it in the right way. Sometimes questions will simply begin 'Why'. These are asking you to analyse the causes of an event or development. For the highest marks you will need to show how factors combined to bring about the event.

Most questions will ask you for a judgment. Here are some different types of question stem you may come across in the exam:

1  How far was x responsible for y?
2  To what extent did x change?
3  How far did x depend on y?
4  Did x play a major part in y?

Although judgment questions come in a variety of forms, they are all asking you to balance points. In the case of example 2 below, you will be looking for evidence of change and of continuity in order to reach a judgment about the extent of change.

When you choose your question in the examination, take note of what sort of judgment it asks you to make. The essay questions test a variety of skills. Here are some examples of different skills being tested by the questions.

1.  The analysis of, and judgment about, the **key features** of a situation.
    For example: *To what extent did the Nazis unite the German people in support of their rule in the years 1933–1939?*
2.  The analysis of, and judgment about, the **extent of change**.
    For example: *How far did Nazi policy towards Germany's Jews change in the years 1933–1941?*
3.  The analysis of **consequences or effects**.
    For example: *How far did the Nazis succeed in achieving the aims of their economic policies in the years 1933–1941?*
4.  The analysis of, and judgment about, the **causes** of a historical event or situation.
    For example: *To what extent were Hitler's errors and misjudgments responsible for Germany's defeat in the Second World War?*

Another type of question will ask you how far you agree with a statement. This is still a judgment question. You should clarify what the statement is about so that you know what the question expects of you.

- Is it a statement about causation, like this question: *How accurate is it to say that the economic slump in Germany was responsible for the remarkable rise in support for the Nazi Party in the years 1928–1932?*
- Or is it about consequence, like this question: *How accurate is it to say that Nazi policies towards women and young people in the years 1933–1939 were completely unsuccessful?*

When you are clear about what the question wants from you, you can use what you have learned in the Skills Builder sections of this book to produce an answer based on extended writing (an essay) which will help you to gain high marks.

# How to revise

## Make a revision plan

Before you start revising, make a plan. Otherwise it is easy to waste your precious revision time. It is helpful to look at your exam dates and work backwards to the first date you intend to start revising. Here are some tips on how to create a revision plan:

1 First, fill in the dates of your examinations and then any regular commitments you have. This will help give you a realistic idea of how much time you have to revise.

2 Plan your time carefully, assigning more time to topics you find difficult.

3 Use a revision 'checklist'. Look at what you need to know and try to identify any gaps in your knowledge.

4 Now fill in the timetable with sensible work slots and breaks.

5 Keep to this timetable! Organise yourself well and it will help you to fulfil your potential. If you have not prepared a revision plan yet, it is not too late to start. Put your plan up somewhere visible so you can refer back to it.

## Revision tips

- Revise often – try to do a little every day.
- Make sure you have one day a week when you don't do revision or even think about exams – you'll come back to it refreshed.
- Take a five- or ten-minute break every hour, and do some stretching exercises, go for a short walk or make a drink.
- Talk to your family or a friend about your revision – they may be able to help you. For example, they could test you on key facts.
- Keep bullet points on 'crib cards', highlighting important revision points. For example, you could have a list or a mind map of the reasons why the Nazis were able to make their electoral breakthrough in the early 1930s. Use these for quick revision and for reading during 'dead' times – when you're waiting for a bus, for example.

- Use mnemonics. This is when you take the first letter of each of a series of words you want to remember and then make a new sentence. A common mnemonic for remembering the order of the points of the compass (North, East, South and West) is 'Naughty Elephants Squirt Water'.

- Some people revise well by listening, so you could try 'talking' your revision and recording it onto an mp3 player if you have one. Listen to the recordings while lying in bed, while travelling in a car or walking to the shops. This also takes the guilt out of being out and about rather than in front of your books!

- Practise your exam techniques. As you revise key topics, plan five or six points to make about the causes/consequences/key features/changes relating to major developments. You could use question stems 1–4 on the previous page, and slot in your own x and y.

- Try doing some timed essays. This will make it easier to write a good essay when it comes to the exam.

- Don't panic. Think about what you can achieve, not what you can't. Positive thinking is important! Remember the examiner will be looking to reward you for what you can do.

# Assessment objectives

To do well in your exam, you need to make sure you meet all the assessment objectives. Below are the assessment objectives you need to meet and some advice on how to make sure you meet them.

## Recall, select and deploy historical knowledge
AO1a

In your essay, you must show that you can remember, choose and use historical knowledge.

- Remember – *recollect historical facts from your study of this unit*
- Choose – *select specific facts that are relevant to the essay you are writing*
- Use – *place these facts in your essay in a way that supports your argument*

## Understanding of the past
AO1b (i)

You need to show that you understand the period studied. Simply telling the story of what happened will not help you to do this. Instead, you need to:

- Analyse – *break down the topic you are considering into key points*
- Explain – *suggest reasons why these key points provide an answer to the question*
- Reach a judgment – *decide which of your key points was most important and provide reasons to support this*

As you think about analysis, explanation and judgment, remember to bear in mind the relevant **key concepts** and **relationships**.

## Key concepts
AO1b (ii)

When faced with an essay question, consider which of the following key concepts it focuses on:

- Causation – *what made an event happen?*
- Consequence – *what were the results of this event?*
- Continuity – *in what ways did things stay the same?*
- Change – *in what ways were things different?*
- Significance – *why was this important?*

Then ensure that your answer remains focused on this concept.

## Relationships
AO1b (iii)

Once you have planned the key points you will make in your essay, consider the following:

- How do these key points link together?
- Which key point was most important? Why?

Once you have considered these issues, arrange your points in an order that reflects the way they link together or the relative importance of each key point.

# Level descriptors

Each essay you write in the exam will be given a mark out of 30 and will correspond to a level from 1 to 5, with level 5 being the highest. Here is some information about what the levels mean. Read it carefully and use this information to aim for the top!

## Level 1:
- General points about the historical period that are correct but not necessarily focused on the topic raised by the question.
- The general points will not be supported by accurate and relevant specific examples.

*Answers at this level will be very simplistic, irrelevant or vague.*

## Level 2:
- A number of general points about the topic of the question.
- The general points will be supported by some accurate and relevant examples.

*Answers at this level might tell the story or part of the story without addressing the question, or might list the key points without backing them up with specific examples.*

## Level 3:
- A number of points with some focus on the question.
- The points will be supported by accurate material, but some whole paragraphs may be either only partly relevant, lacking in detail or both.

*At Level 3 answers will attempt to focus on the question and have some strengths (some paragraphs will have point, supporting evidence and linkage back to the question), but answers will also have significant areas of weakness. For example, the focus on the question may drift, the answer may lack specific examples or parts of the essay may simply tell the story.*

## Level 4:
- A number of points which clearly address the question and show an understanding of the most important factors involved.
- The points will be supported by accurate material which will be mostly relevant and detailed.
- There will be clear explanation of how the points and specific examples provide an answer to the question.

*At Level 4 answers will clearly attempt to tackle the question and demonstrate a detailed knowledge of the period studied.*

## Level 5:
- A number of points which clearly address the question and show a thorough understanding of the most important factors involved.
- The points will be supported by accurate material which will be relevant and detailed.
- There will be clear explanation of how the points and specific examples provide an answer to the question, as well as an evaluation of the relative importance of the different factors or issues discussed.

*Answers that are judged to be Level 5 will be thorough and detailed – they will clearly engage with the specific question, providing a balanced and carefully reasoned argument that reaches a clear and supported judgment.*

# Sample answer 1

## How far was there economic and political stability in Germany in the years 1924–1929?

**[30 marks available]**

### An answer given a mark in Level 5 of the published mark scheme

There was economic and political stability in the years 1924-1929 to the extent that these years are regarded as the 'golden years' of Weimar. However, it can be seen that Germany was in fact 'dancing on a volcano' through the massive injection of loans which it could not afford to repay.

### EXAMINER COMMENT

A crisp, clear-minded start which focuses precisely on the terms of the question set and which shows that the candidate understands that although the Weimar Republic was more stable after 1924 than it had been previously it also had continuing, deep-rooted problems. This introduction indicates that what will follow is a balanced discussion in which elements of both stability and instability will be considered.

The Weimar constitution is important in considering the stability of Germany as a nation. The constitution was introduced in June 1919 - the same date as the Treaty of Versailles. This was the ultimate milestone in Germany's humiliation, with harsh clauses, such as Article 231, the war guilt clause. The circumstances in which the constitution was introduced meant instability from the very start, due to the fact that right-wing nationalists were always going to be opposed to the Republic, holding it responsible for the humiliating defeat of Germany.

### EXAMINER COMMENT

This is not as clear and well-directed as the opening paragraph, but it does make the valuable point that Germany's extreme right was a serious destabilising influence throughout the 1920s.

However, it can be argued that Germany experienced a striking recovery after the hyperinflation of 1923. The introduction of the Rentenmark provided stability for Germany's currency contributing to the economic recovery after 1924. Economic recovery promoted political stability. This can be seen in the election results of the later 1920s. In the elections of April 1924, the Nazis gained seats, winning 7 percent of the vote. In the following elections in December 1924, the Nazi vote went down to 3 percent, while in the 1928 elections the Nazis were humiliated with just 2 percent of the vote and only 12 seats in the Reichstag. The elections indicated increased political stability, with the extreme parties unable to make an impact.

### EXAMINER COMMENT

This paragraph offers evidence of economic and political stability in Germany after 1924. It links the two convincingly and it offers well-selected and impressively detailed evidence of increased political stability.

Moreover, proportional representation contributed to economic stability, though whether it was a positive force for political stability is a question. The proportional voting system enabled small moderate parties to contribute in the Reichstag and in government, something which would not have happened under the British 'first-past-the-post' system. Proportional representation was ultimately a weakness of the Weimar Republic. This is proved by the existence of twenty coalition governments between 1919 and 1933. At the same time, it should be remembered that Weimar was one of the most democratic political systems in Europe. It can be argued that the Weimar Republic as a political system was relatively stable in the years 1924-1928 despite proportional representation, but the economic slump of 1929 proved fatal to it.

## EXAMINER COMMENT

This paragraph addresses the difficult question of the extent to which Weimar Germany's voting system was a cause of its political instability. It is arguably the least satisfactory paragraph in the answer. The writing lacks a clear sense of direction and the reasoning is not always secure. For example, no explanation is offered in support of the claim that proportional representation helped to bring about economic stability. The paragraph does, however, demonstrate an awareness of the fact that Weimar Germany suffered from the problem of weak, short-lived coalition governments throughout its existence.

In terms of economic stability after 1924, the most important person in Germany's politics was Gustav Stresemann. In the role of Foreign Minister, Stresemann in 1924 negotiated the Dawes Plan with the Allies. This provided massive injections of loans from the USA and it allowed Germany to begin its economic recovery from the chaos of World War I. The loans led to an increase in production and a decrease in unemployment. Confidence within Germany revived. However, if the whole ambiguous picture is looked at, it can be seen that economic recovery was only short-term.

In fact, Germany was in Stresemann's words 'dancing on a volcano'. Stability was dependent on foreign wealth. The withdrawal of these loans meant collapse. This is what happened after the Wall Street Crash of 1929. Moreover, economic stability was related to political stability. The economic downturn led to a loss of confidence in democratic politicians as the middle-class parties and the Social Democrats were unable to reach agreement on how to tackle the economic slump. Germany once more became a failed state. Stresemann could see that Germany's economic stability did not have solid foundations and so can the historian.

## EXAMINER COMMENT

These two paragraphs further explore the basis of, and extent of, economic stability in Germany after 1924. They relate closely to the question set; they offer a well-founded judgment on the extent to which Germany was economically stable in the later 1920s; and the points made are effectively supported with evidence.

One of the things that contributed to political instability in Germany after 1924 was the President. It is true that Hindenburg was elected to the Presidency in 1925 with public support. But the fact that the aristocrat Hindenburg was President with Article 48 at his command meant that democracy was again under threat. However, within the given years 1924-1929 Hindenburg did not misuse Article 48 to threaten the democratic system. Democracy survived even though the President was not a democrat.

The Young Plan of 1929, negotiated by Stresemann, was in some ways a victory for Germany due to the fact that the reparations bill was reduced. However, it was also an acceptance of defeat by Germany in that it agreed to pay reparations for years to come. This presented extreme right-wing groups with a perfect opportunity to inflict a political defeat on the Weimar Republic. Right-wing nationalists like Hitler and Hugenberg campaigned to have the burdens of the Versailles Treaty lifted. Their campaign against the Young Plan gained massive publicity. This was evidence of political instability.

In 1919-1923 there were 354 political murders in Germany. Violence of this kind did not occur during the 'golden years'. However, it was replaced by violence of a different kind. In the late 1920s there were numerous street fights between the Nazi Brownshirts and the Communists with the Nazis claiming that Germany was under threat from the 'Red Peril'. This violence was evidence of political instability.

## EXAMINER COMMENT

These three paragraphs are linked in that they deal with three different aspects of political instability in late 1920s Germany: the election of an anti-democrat as President in 1925; the campaign against the Young Plan in 1929; and the ongoing problem of political violence. Each paragraph makes a relevant and well-founded point which is effectively supported with evidence. Together these three paragraphs on political instability balance the discussion earlier in the essay where the focus was largely on increased stability after 1924.

It can be seen that the political and economic situation of Germany improved during 1924-1929 due to the remarkable input of Stresemann. Whether or not Germany was a lot more stable economically after 1924 is open to question. It was economically stable to the extent that life in Germany improved in comparison with the years before 1924 but not to the extent that it could last forever. Germany lost the battle with the volcano. Politically, things were better after 1924 but there was still a lot of evidence of instability.

## EXAMINER COMMENT

This is not an unblemished essay. There are some uncertain passages and it is better developed on political stability than it is on economic stability. It does, however, have a number of very clear strengths: it focuses tightly on the question set more or less throughout; it offers a balanced analysis of the extent of economic and political stability in 1924–1929; and the points made are supported by relevant and detailed evidence. This answer deserves a Level 5 mark (28 marks out of a possible 30 marks).

# Sample answer 2

## How far was there economic and political stability in Germany in the years 1924–1929?
## [30 marks available]

### An answer given a mark in Level 3 of the published mark scheme

During the years 1924-1929, there was a boost in Germany's fortunes. After 1924, people's lives had begun to improve. Although the Treaty of Versailles had been harsh, the government at the time - Stresemann in particular - had made a series of negotiations that allowed Germany some legroom. These negotiations came about after Germany declared itself bankrupt and could no longer afford to pay reparations, which then prompted the French to enter the Rhineland and use the area's natural resources. Stresemann's negotiations involved the French leaving the Rhineland, and also the USA, in that the President allowed them generous loans in order to rebuild their economy. This allowed Germans to begin to build up the declining economy once more, and this allowed people the stability they needed to begin to take out loans, start businesses and begin to save. In essence, the Germans were beginning to flourish.

## EXAMINER COMMENT

This paragraph does not set out what the candidate plans to cover and discuss in the main body of the essay which follows. Instead it jumps straight in to a discussion of the reasons for Germany's increased economic stability after 1924. Much of what is said on this point is well-founded but there are factual inaccuracies. Germany did not declare itself bankrupt in early 1923 and the French occupied the Ruhr, not the Rhineland. Furthermore, much of this material is not directly focused on the question, which asks for an assessment of whether Germany was stable. It is also a little long for an introductory paragraph.

Politically, from 1924, it could be argued that these were the Weimar Republic's 'golden years' in that the government, despite the coalitions, was doing a good job, and fewer and fewer people were interested in extremist parties such as Hitler's NSDAP. The Centre Party, the SPD and the Catholic Party, which helped to make up the government, were introducing policies which were pleasing people. For example, jobs were on the increase.

## EXAMINER COMMENT

This paragraph focuses on the relative political stability of Germany in the years 1924–1929. It rightly draws attention to the success of the moderate parties in the later 1920s and to the decline in support for the extreme right-wing parties. It does not, though, offer any evidence to support its claim that the government introduced popular policies. There is also uncertainty concerning the political parties of Weimar Germany: the 'Centre Party' and 'the Catholic Party' were not different political parties as is suggested.

However, on 29 October 1929, the Wall Street Crash occurred, which changed the face of Germany both economically and politically. Politically, the coalition was a mess. The differing parties could not make a decision on how their electorate would be affected, and thus the Weimar Republic began to crumble. Economically, Germans were ruined. As the USA was hit terribly, it began to try to claw back money by recalling its loans to Germany. This left Germany in an even worse position: money that people had carefully saved was now worthless, and businesses were hit hardest. It has been estimated that up to 1 million people died of starvation. Worst of all, the 'Grand Coalition' could not do much to stop the suffering of the population, as each party was trying to make their own party voters comfortable.

## EXAMINER COMMENT

This paragraph describes the destabilising effects of the 1929 economic slump on Germany. It displays some knowledge and understanding of the reasons why Germany was so badly affected by the world economic depression. The explanation is not, however, always clearly worded, and there are signs as well of limited understanding. Germany did not experience inflation after 1929 – as is suggested – but deflation.

In conclusion, during the years 1924 to 1929, Germany began on a rise, starting to get a better economy and political stability, as well as a better life for most Germans. However, the Wall Street Crash meant that the political parties were at a loss, and the failing economy brought about hardship.

## EXAMINER COMMENT

This essay tries to focus on the question set and displays some knowledge and understanding of increased economic and political stability in Germany after 1924. There is some attempt at analysis, but the essay is essentially narrative in form, telling the story of post-1924 improvement and post-1929 collapse. The supporting evidence is limited and the issue of the extent of economic and political stability in 1924–1929 is not explicitly addressed. In view of these significant areas of weakness, this essay would be awarded a Level 3 (14 marks out of a possible 30 marks).

# Index

Published by Pearson Education Limited, a company incorporated in England and Wales, having its registered office at Edinburgh Gate, Harlow, Essex, CM20 2JE. Registered company number: 872828

www.pearsonschoolsandfecolleges.co.uk

Edexcel is a registered trademark of Edexcel Limited

Text © Pearson Education Limited 2010

The rights of Alan White have been asserted by him in accordance with the Copyright, Designs and Patents Act 1988.

First published 2010

15

10 9 8 7 6 5

**British Library Cataloguing in Publication Data**
A catalogue record for this book is available from the British Library

ISBN 978 1 84690 752 4

Edited by Polly Hennessy
Typeset by Ian Foulis
Original illustrations © Pearson Education 2010
Illustrated by Ian Foulis
Printed in Malaysia, CTP-PJB

**Acknowledgements**
The author and publisher would like to thank the following for their kind permission to reproduce their photographs:
(Key: b-bottom; c-centre; l-left; r-right; t-top)

**Bridgeman Art Library Ltd:** Private Collection / Look and Learn 55; **Bundesarchiv-Bildarchiv:** 6, 27, 39, 50, 51, 52, 53, 61, 64, 65, 82, 92, 93; **Mary Evans Picture Library:** 20; **Getty Images:** 14, 89; L. **Orgel-Köhne/DHM, Berlin:** 74

**Cover images:** *Front:* **Bridgeman Art Library Ltd:** Private Collection / Look and Learn

All other images © Pearson Education

The author and publisher would like to thank the following individuals and organisations for permission to reproduce copyrighted material:

Table on page 80 adapted from *The Longman Companion to Nazi Germany*, Longman (Kirk, T. 1995) p. 94, with permission from Pearson Education Ltd; Table on page 93 adapted from *The Penguin Historical Atlas of the Third Reich*, Penguin Books (Overy, R. 1996) p. 132, Copyright ©) Richard Overy 1966. Reproduced by permission of Penguin Books Ltd; Table on page 94 adapted from *World War II Data Book: Third Reich, 1933-1945*, Amber Books Ltd. (McNab, C. 2009) p. 59; Table on page 95 adapted from *Why the Allies Won*, Copyright © 2004 Richard Overy. From *Why the Allies Won* now published by Pimlico. Reproduced by permission of the author c/o Rogers, Coleridge & White Ltd., 20 Powis Mews, London W11 1JN. Reprinted by permission of The Random House Group Ltd., Copyright © 1995 by Richard Overy.  Used by permission of W.W. Norton & Company, Inc.

Details of written sources:
Extract on page 69 from *The Nuremberg Interviews*, Pimlico (Goldensohn, L. (ed.) 2004) p. 300, reprinted by permission of The Random House Group Ltd.

In some instances we have been unable to trace the owners of copyright material, and we would appreciate any information that would enable us to do so.

Tables on pages 16, 21 and 43 from *Weimar Republic*, Collins Educational (White, A. 1997). Table on p. 84 from *Nazism 1919-1945, Volume 2: State, Economy and Society, 1933-1939*, Exeter University Press (Noakes, J. and Pridham, G. 1984), p. 292

Every effort has been made to trace the copyright holders and we apologise in advance for any unintentional omissions. We would be pleased to insert the appropriate acknowledgement in any subsequent edition of this publication.

**Websites**

The websites used in this book were correct and up-to-date at the time of publication. It is essential for tutors to preview each website before using it in class so as to ensure that the URL is still accurate, relevant and appropriate. We suggest that tutors bookmark useful websites and consider enabling students to access them through the school/college intranet.

**Disclaimer**

This material has been published on behalf of Edexcel and offers high-quality support for the delivery of Edexcel qualifications. This does not mean that the material is essential to achieve any Edexcel qualification, nor does it mean that it is the only suitable material available to support any Edexcel qualification. Edexcel material will not be used verbatim in setting any Edexcel examination or assessment. Any resource lists produced by Edexcel shall include this and other appropriate resources.

Copies of official specifications for all Edexcel qualifications may be found on the Edexcel website: www.edexcel.com.